Test Prep Wo
PROVIDES A NEW APPROACH TO MATERIALS

Are you an education professional?

You know your students. You know the test.

Shouldn't your materials reflect that?

The Test Prep Works advantages include:

- A low, one-time set up fee with no minimum purchases
- Buy only the books that you need, when you need them
- Access to the Test Prep Works tutoring forum where you can exchange ideas with other tutors and request additional materials

TEST PREP WORKS

CAN PROVIDE MATERIALS FOR

YOUR SCHOOL OR TUTORING

COMPANY. WE OFFER THE ABILITY

TO CUSTOMIZE OUR MATERIALS TO

REFLECT THE IDENTITY OF YOUR

SCHOOL OR COMPANY.

Please visit www.TestPrepWorks.com for more information

30 Days

TO *ACING* THE
UPPER LEVEL SSAT

Strategies and Practice for Maximizing
Your Upper Level SSAT Score

Christa Abbott, M.Ed.

Published by:
Test Prep Works, LLC
741 N. Danville St.
Arlington, VA 22201
www.TestPrepWorks.com

SSAT is a registered trademark of the Secondary School Admission Test Board. They have not endorsed nor are they associated with this book.

Neither the author nor the publisher of this book claims responsibility for the accuracy of this book or the outcome of students who use these materials.

ISBN 978-1-939090-00-3

Table of Contents

About the Author 7

About Test Prep Works, LLC 8

How To Use This Book 9

The 30-Day to SSAT Success Game Plan 10

What You Need To Know For the SSAT—Just the Basics 11

The Format of the Upper Level SSAT 13

Quantitative Sections—Basic Strategies 15

Verbal Section—Basic Strategies 21

Reading Comprehension Section—Basic Strategies 31

Now that you have the strategies, it is time to head to the workouts! 36

Workout #1 38

Workout #1 Answers 45

Workout #2 48

Workout #2 Answers 55

Workout #3 59

Workout #3 Answers 66

Workout #4 69

Answers to Workout #4 78

Workout #5 81

Answers to Workout #5 90

Workout #6 93

Answers to Workout #6 101

Workout #7 104

Answers to Workout #7 112

Workout #8 115

Answers to Workout #8 122

Workout #9 126

Answers to Workout #9 134

Workout #10 138

Workout #10 Answers 146

Workout #11 149

Workout #11 Answers 156

Workout #12 159

Workout #12 Answers 166

Workout #13 169

Workout #13 Answers 176

Workout #14 179

Workout #14 Answers 185

Workout #15 188

Workout #15 Answers 195

Appendix A 197

About the Author

Christa Abbott has been working as a private test prep tutor for over a decade. She has worked with students who have been admitted to and attended some of the top independent schools in the country. Over the years, she has developed materials for each test that truly make the difference. She is a graduate of Middlebury College and received her Masters in Education from the University of Virginia, a program nationally known for its excellence. Her background in education allows her to develop materials based on the latest research about how we learn so that preparation can be effective and an efficient use of time. Her materials are also designed to be developmentally appropriate for the ages of the students taking the tests. In her free time, she enjoys hiking, tennis, Scrabble, and reading.

Christa continues to coach students one-on-one in the Washington, D.C., area as well as students all over the world via the internet. If you are interested in these services, please visit www.ChristaAbbott.com.

About Test Prep Works, LLC

Test Prep Works, LLC, was founded to provide effective materials for test preparation. Its founder, Christa Abbott, spent years looking for effective materials for the private school entrance exams but came up empty-handed. The books available combined several different tests and while there are overlaps, they are not the same test. Christa found this to be very, very overwhelming for students who were in elementary and middle school and that just didn't seem necessary. Christa developed her own materials to use with students that are specific for each level of the test and are not just adapted from other books. For the first time, these materials are available to the general public as well as other tutors. Please visit *www.TestPrepWorks.com* to view a complete array of offerings as well as sign up for a newsletter with recent news and developments in the world of admissions and test preparation.

How To Use This Book

This book is designed to teach you what you need to know in order to maximize your upper level SSAT performance. The book starts with a brief introduction to strategies for each section. After that, there are a series of "workouts". Each of these workouts should take you no longer than 30-40 minutes each.

Within each workout, I have included practice problems from each section of the test so that you get a "balanced diet" leading up to test day. You will notice some repetition- this is by design! In particular, you may see vocabulary words or words with the same roots repeated. This is to ensure that you really know these words since they are the words that crop up again and again on the SSAT. Also, be sure to check your answers and figure out WHY you missed the questions that you did. The analysis is as important as the answers themselves.

I have spent years studying the test and analyzing the different question types, content, and the types of answers that the test writers prefer. Now you can benefit from my hard work! I will show how to approach questions so that you can raise your score significantly in just 30-40 minutes a day.

Let's get started!

P.S. I chose not to go into the nitty gritty details in this book about how to register, what to bring on test day, etc., because I want you to focus just on strategies and practice for now. Make sure to visit *www.SSAT.org* to get all of the current details on registration and other procedures. I also highly recommend ordering their practice book, "Preparing and Applying to Independent School". It has two practice tests in it that you can complete after you finish all of the workouts.

P.P.S. If you are looking for a complete course, phone apps, and other study materials, please visit *www.TestPrepWorks.com*

The 30-Day to SSAT Success Game Plan

Step 1: Read Through the Strategy Section of this Book

Take the time to really understand each strategy, but know that what you have learned will be reinforced in the workouts.

Step 2: Complete the Workouts

When you miss a question, take the time to understand WHY you missed it before you move on to the next workout. Make flashcards for words and roots that you don't know and study them as you go.

Step 3: Read the Appendix

It gives advice on how to tackle the writing sample

Step 4: Take the Practice Tests

Order the book "Preparing and Applying for Independent School". (Please note that the ONLY place you can get this book is from *www.ssat.org*). Take the Upper Level practice tests using the strategies that you have learned. Understand why you missed the questions that you did.

Step 5: Rock out the SSAT

What You Need To Know For the SSAT—Just the Basics

Here is what you really need to know to do well on the Upper Level SSAT:

✓ How the Scoring Works

On the Upper Level SSAT, if you get a question correct, then you are given one point. If you answer a question and get it wrong, then they subtract a quarter point. If you don't answer at all, then you don't get a point added to your raw score, but they don't take off a quarter point, either.

You might be asking why they use this crazy system. The thinking behind it is that on a regular test, you would get ahead by guessing. You would get some of the questions that you guessed on correct and therefore your score would be higher for blindly guessing. Actually, chances are you would get 1/5 of the questions correct if you blindly guessed because there are five answer choices for each question. By taking off a quart point for the 4/5 of the questions that you missed, the test writers are just making sure that you don't get ahead for guessing.

If you think this sounds way too complicated, the SSATB (the people who publish the test) agree. As of the writing of this book (fall 2012), this scoring system is still in place. However, they will be working on phasing it out. As early as 2013 they might not be taking off a quarter point if you get a question wrong. Please, please, please check *www.TestPrepWorks.com* or *www.SSAT.org* to confirm how the scoring will work. I will update this book when the change is made, but you may be working with an older copy.

✓ When To Guess

As long as the above scoring policy is in place, you should only guess if you can rule out one answer choice. Once the policy changes, you should answer everything, even if you haven't looked at the question.

✓ What Schools Are *Really* Looking For and the Beauty of the Percentile Score

You will get a raw score for the SSAT based upon how many questions you get right or wrong. This raw score will then be converted into a scaled score. Neither of these scores are what schools are really looking at. They are looking for your percentile scores, and in particular the percentile scores that compare you to other students applying to independent school.

The percentile score compares you to other students of the same gender that are in your grade. For example, let's say that you are an eighth grade boy and you scored in the 70th percentile. What this means is that out of a hundred boys in your grade, you would have done better than 70 of them.

Keep in mind that the Upper Level SSAT is given to students up through 11th grade. That means that if you are taking the test in 8th grade, there could very well be some material on the test that you simply have not yet covered. You may miss some of these questions, but as long as the other students your age also miss them, then it won't affect your percentile score.

Many students applying to independent schools are used to getting almost all the questions correct on a test. You will probably miss more questions on this test than you are used to missing, but because the percentile score is what schools are looking at, don't let it get to you.

The Format of the Upper Level SSAT

You can expect to see four scored sections *plus* a writing sample *plus* an experimental section on the Upper Level SSAT.

The four scored sections are:

✓ **Quantitative (there will be two of these sections on your test)**

- A variety of math problems

- Each section has 25 problems, for a total of 50 math problems

- 30 minutes to complete each section, or a little more than a minute per problem

✓ **Verbal**

- 30 synonym questions and 30 analogy questions

- 30 minutes to complete the section, or about 30 seconds per question

✓ **Reading Comprehension**

- Passages and questions

- Passages can be fiction, non-fiction, and poetry

- A total of 40 questions

- Generally 6-8 passages, each passage having 4-8 questions, but this is not carved in stone so you may see some variation

- 40 minutes to complete section

The four above sections are all multiple choice. Each question has five answer choices.

The Experimental Section

✓ This is new for fall of 2012. It is supposed to be 15 minutes long and will NOT contribute to your score

✓ SSATB is just trying out new problems for future tests, not to worry

The Writing Sample

✓ Will NOT be scored, but a copy will be sent to all of the schools that you apply to

✓ In the summer of 2012, the SSATB changed the format of the writing section. You will now be able to choose one of two writing prompts, one will be fiction and one will be an essay

✓ 25 minutes to write and you will be given two pages to write on

Now, on to the strategies! The strategies covered in this book will focus on the multiple choice sections since those are what is used to determine your percentile. Please see the appendix for tips on the essay before test day.

Quantitative Sections— Basic Strategies

On the quantitative sections, there are problems from arithmetic, algebra, and geometry. The math is really not that hard. The SSAT is more about figuring out what concepts they are testing than remembering complicated equations.

You will NOT be allowed to use a calculator on the SSAT. Yes, you read that correctly. By using strategies, however, we can get to the right answers, often without using complicated calculations.

The goal here is for you to get a general understanding of the key strategies for the math section. The workouts are where you will practice these strategies and work on content.

Drumroll, please! The strategies are:

- ✓ Use estimating- this is a multiple choice test!

- ✓ If there are variables in the answer choices, try plugging in your own numbers. If it is a "must be true" question, try plugging in weird numbers such as negatives, zero, and fractions

- ✓ If they ask for the value of a variable, plug in answer choices

- ✓ If you can, find a range that the answer should fall within

Strategy #1: Use Estimating

You can spend a lot of time finding the exact right answer on this test, or you can spend time figuring out what answers couldn't possibly work and then choose from what is left.

For example, let's say the question is:

$$72,341 \div 2281 =$$

1. The answer to above equation is closest to which of the following?
    (A) 72,000
    (B) 70,000
    (C) 36,000
    (D) 360
    (E) 36

If you were to do out the whole problem, that would take a long time without a calculator. However, if we look at our answer choices, we can see that most of them are pretty spread out. We just need to know roughly what the answer would be, so we can do *72,000÷2,000*, which gives us 36, or answer choice E.

You can use estimating on many of the problems, but in particular estimate when the question uses the words "closest to" or "approximately".

Strategy #2: Plug in your own numbers if there are variables in the answer choices

What do I mean by variables in the answer choices? If you look at the answer choices and some or all of them have letters in addition to numbers, then you have variables in your answer choices.

Here is how this strategy works:

1. Make up your own numbers for the variables. Just make sure they work within the problem. If they say that x is less than 1, do not make x equal to 2! If they say $x+y=1$, then for heavens sake, don't make x equal to 2 and y equal to 3. Also, make sure that you write down what you are plugging in for your variables. EVERY TIME. You think you will remember that x was 4, but then you go to try out answer choices and it gets all confused. Just write it down the first time. Also, try to avoid using -1, 1, and 0 because they have funky properties and you might get more than one answer that works. The exception to this rule is when the question asks you what *must* be true. In that case, you want to use the funky numbers to try to rule out answer choices.

2. Solve the problem using your numbers. Write down the number that you get and circle it. This is the number you are trying to get with your answer choices when you plug in your value for the variable.

3. Plug the numbers that you assigned to the variables in step 1 into the answer choices and see which answer choice matches the number that you circled.

Here is an example:

1. Each mama mouse can have up to 9 baby mice in a litter. What is the maximum total number of mice that could wind up in a cage if there are x mama mice in the cage?
    (A) $x + 9$
    (B) $9x$
    (C) $9x + 9$
    (D) $10x$
    (E) $10x + 10$

Step 1: Plug in our own number.

Let's make x equal to 3. We now have 3 mama mice.

Step 2: Solve using our own numbers.

If we have 3 mama mice, and they could each have nine babies, then the total number of mice we could wind up with in our cage is 30. We write down this number and circle it.

Step 3: Plug into answer choices.

We are looking for the answer choice that would be equal to 30.
    (A) $3 + 9 = 12$
    (B) $9(3) = 27$
    (C) $9(3) + 9 = 36$
    (D) $10(3) = 30$
    (E) $10(3) + 10 = 40$

Choice D gives us 30, which is what we were looking for, so we choose D and get the question correct.

If the question asks you which answer choice is greatest or least, then you won't come up with a target number to circle. Rather, you will just plug your values into the answer choices and see which one is greatest or least, depending on what the question asked for.

Here is an example:

1. If x is less than 0, and y is greater than 1, which of the following is GREATEST?

   (A) $x - y$

   (B) $\frac{x-y}{2}$

   (C) $\frac{1}{x}$

   (D) $\frac{1}{y}$

   (E) $y - x$

Step 1: Choose our own numbers.

Let's make $x = -1$ and $y = 2$. These are nice round numbers and work with the limits given by the problem.

Step 2: Plug into answer choices and see what gives us the GREATEST number

   (A) $x - y = -1 - 2 = -3$

   (B) $\frac{x-y}{2} = \frac{-1-2}{2} = -\frac{3}{2}$

   (C) $\frac{1}{x} = \frac{1}{-1} = -1$

   (D) $\frac{1}{y} = \frac{1}{2}$

   (E) $y - x = 2 - (-1) = 2 + 1 = 3$

By plugging in our own numbers, we can clearly see that choice E gives us the GREATEST number, so we choose choice E and get it right!

One thing to note about the strategy of plugging in is that you can use it even when they ask what must be true or what is always true. Just keep plugging in different numbers to the answer choices until you have ruled out all but one answer choice.

Strategy #3: If they ask for the value of a variable, plug in answer choices

For this strategy, keep in mind that a variable is not always a letter. The problem might define x as the number of cars, or it might just ask you what the number of cars is. Either way, it is still asking for the value of a variable and you can use this strategy.

Here is how you use this strategy:

Step 1: Put your answer choices in order from least to greatest if they are not already in that order

Step 2: Plug the middle answer choice into the problem to see if it works

Step 3: If the middle choice does not work, go bigger or smaller depending on what you got for the middle answer choice

Here is an example:

1. A fence is going to be built around a cow pasture. The width of the fenced-in area is to be half the length of the fenced-in area. If the farmer uses exactly 24 yards of fencing, what is the width of the fenced-in area?
    (A)   1 yard
    (B)   2 yards
    (C)   3 yards
    (D)   4 yards
    (E)   8 yards

    In this case, the answer choices are already in order (they usually are), so we can skip step 1 and go right to step 2.

Step 2: Plug in middle answer choice.

In this case, we make the width equal to 3 in order to test out answer choice C. If the width was 3 yards, then the length would be 6 yards. If we add 2 widths and 2 lengths, then we would get a perimeter of 18 yards. The problem tells us that the distance around should be 24, however, so we know that choice C does not work. Not only do we know that choice C does not work, but we also know that we need a longer width in order to get a perimeter of 24 yards.

Step 3: Go bigger or smaller if the middle answer choice did not work

Next, we make the width 4 yards in order to test out choice D. If the width was 4 yards, then the length would be 8 yards. If we add 2 widths and 2 lengths to get the perimeter, then the perimeter in this case would be 24 yards. That is exactly the distance around that the problem gave us, so we know that choice D is correct.

Strategy #4: If you can, find a range that the answer should fall within

Since you are not allowed to use a calculator on this test, try to see if you can at least figure out what two numbers an answer should fall in between.

Here is an example:

1. $90 - 6\frac{7}{18} =$

    (A) $82\frac{11}{18}$

    (B) $83\frac{11}{18}$

    (C) $84\frac{7}{18}$

    (D) $84\frac{11}{18}$

    (E) $85\frac{11}{18}$

To solve this problem, I could do a lot of math. Or I could figure out what numbers the answer should fall in between and then use the fact that this is a multiple choice test to my advantage.

The number $6\frac{7}{18}$ falls in between 6 and 7. $90-6=84$ and $90-7=83$. That tells me that my answer should fall in between 83 and 84. Only answer choice B does, so that is the correct answer.

Those are the basics that you need to know for the math section. As you go through the workouts, you will learn content and the strategies that work for specific problem types.

Verbal Section—
Basic Strategies

In the verbal section you will see two question types:

- ✓ Synonyms
- ✓ Analogies

On the synonym questions, you will be given one question word and then you have to choose the answer choice that has the word that comes closest in meaning to the question word.

Synonym questions look something like this:

1. JOYOUS
   - (A) loud
   - (B) crying
   - (C) happy
   - (D) shy
   - (E) lame

Out of all the answer choice words, happy comes closest in meaning to joyous. Choice C is correct.

The synonyms questions probably won't be quite this easy, but you get the idea.

The analogies questions generally give you two words and you have to figure out the relationship between them and then choose the answer choice that has the same relationship.

The analogy questions usually look something like this:

1. Panther is to cat as
   (A) lion is to jungle
   (B) wolf is to dog
   (C) chick is to bluejay
   (D) mouse is to guinea pig
   (E) horse is to cow

In this case, a panther is a wild cat. A wolf is a wild dog, so choice B is correct.

Sometimes, you will be given the first word in the answer relationship and you just have to choose the second word.

These questions look like this:

1. Tall is to short as narrow is to
   (A) long
   (B) square
   (C) wide
   (D) measured
   (E) lax

Tall and short are opposites, so we are looking for the answer choice that is the opposite of narrow. Wide is the opposite of narrow, so choice C is correct.

Since synonym and analogy questions are very different, we use different strategies for them.

Synonym strategies

✓ Come up with your own word

✓ Is it positive or negative?

✓ Can you think of a sentence or phrase in which you have heard the word?

✓ Are there any roots or word parts that you recognize?

✓ If you have to guess, see if there is an answer choice that has the same prefix, suffix or root as the question word

Strategy #1: Come up with your own word

Use this strategy when you read through a sentence and a word just pops into your head. Don't force yourself to try to come up with your own definition when you aren't sure what the word means.

If you read a question word and a synonym pops into your head, go ahead and jot it down. It is important that you write down the word because otherwise you may try to talk yourself into an answer choice that "seems to come close". One of the biggest enemies on any standardized test is doubt. Doubt leads to talking yourself into the wrong answer, and physically writing down the word gives you the confidence you need when you go through the answer choices.

After you write down the word, start by crossing out answer choices that are not synonyms for your word. By the time you get down to two choices, you will have a much better idea of what you are looking for.

Strategy #2: Using positive or negative

Sometimes you see a word, and you couldn't define that word, but you have a "gut feeling" that it is either something good or something bad. Maybe you don't know what that word means, but you know you would be mad if someone called you that!

To use this strategy, when you get that feeling that a word is either positive or negative, then write in a + or a – sign next to the word. Then go to your answer choices and rule out anything that is opposite, i.e., positive when your question word is negative or negative when your question word is positive.

To really make this strategy work for you, you also need to rule out any words that are neutral, or neither positive nor negative. For example, let's say the question word is DISTRESS. Distress is clearly a negative word. So we could rule out a positive answer choice, such as friendly, but we can also rule out a neutral word, such as sleepy. At night, it is good to be sleepy, during the day it is not. Sleepy is not clearly a negative word, so it goes.

Here is an example:

1. CONDEMN:
   (A) arrive
   (B) blame
   (C) tint
   (D) favor
   (E) laugh

Let's say that you know that condemn is bad, but you can't think of a definition. We write a – sign next to it and then rule out anything that is positive. That means that choices D and E can go because they are both positive. Now we can also rule out neutral words because we know condemn has to be negative. Arrive and tint are neither positive nor negative, so choices A and C are out. We are left with choice B, which is correct.

Strategy #3: Use context-
Think of where you have heard the word before

Use this strategy when you can't define a word, but you can think of a sentence or phrase where you have heard the word before.

Here is how it works: Think of a sentence or phrase where you have heard the question word before. Then try plugging the answer choices into your phrase to see which one has the same meaning within that sentence or phrase.

Here is an example:

1. SHIRK
   (A) rush
   (B) send
   (C) learn
   (D) avoid
   (E) clutter

Now let's say you have heard the word "shirk" but can't define it. You remember your mom telling you "don't shirk your responsibilities" when you tried to watch TV before your chores were done. So we plug in the answer choices for the word shirk in your sentence. Does it make sense to say "don't rush your responsibilities"? It might make sense, but it wouldn't have the same meaning as your context. You weren't in trouble for rushing your chores, you were in trouble for not doing them at all so we can rule out choice A. Does it make sense to say "don't send your responsibilities"? Not at all.

Choice B is out. Does "don't learn your responsibilities" work? Nope, choice C is out. Would your mom say "don't avoid your responsibilities"? You bet. Choice D is correct.

Sometimes the only word or phrase that you can think of uses a different form of the word. That is OK as long as you change the answer choices when you plug in.

Here is an example:

1. CHERISH:
    (A) treasure
    (B) enforce
    (C) utter
    (D) concern
    (E) calm

Maybe you have heard your English teacher talk about *Little Women* as "one of my most cherished books." We can use that context, we just have to add the –ed to the answer choices when we plug them in. Does it make sense to say "one of my most treasured books"? Yes, it does, so we will keep choice A. Would "one of my most enforced books" work? No, so we can rule out choice B. What about "one of my most uttered books" or "one of my most concerned books" or "one of my most calmed books"? No, no, and no, so we rule out choices C, D, and E. Choice A is correct.

Strategy #4: Look for roots or word parts that you know

This strategy works when you recognize that a word looks like another word that you know or when you recognize one of the roots that you have studied in school or in the workouts in this book.

If you see something familiar in the question word, underline the roots or word parts that you recognize. If you can think of the meaning of the root, then look for answer choices that would go with that meaning. If you can't think of a specific meaning, think of other words that have that root and look for answer choices that are similar in meaning to those other words.

Here is an example:

1. EXCLUDE:
   (A) prohibit
   (B) feel
   (C) rest
   (D) drift
   (E) rejoice

There are two word parts in the word "exclude" that can help us out. First, we have the prefix ex-, which means out (think of the word exit). Secondly, clu is a word root that means to shut (think of the word include). Using these word parts, we can see that exclude has something to do with shutting out. Choice A comes closest to this meaning, so it is correct.

Strategy #5: Guess an answer choice with the same prefix, suffix, or word root as the question word

If nothing else, see if any of the answer choices have the same root, prefix, or suffix (a suffix is an ending on a word). You would be amazed how many of the correct answers have the same root as the question word.

Let's look at the following example:

1. PERMISSIBLE
   (A) edible
   (B) crazy
   (C) strong
   (D) allowable
   (E) gentle

Even if you don't know what permissible means, the –ible ending tells us that it must mean able to do something. The –ible and –able suffixes have the same meaning, so we could guess between choices A and D. Edible means able to be eaten, but allowable is a synonym for permissible, so choice D is correct.

Strategies for the Analogies Section

✓ If you know the question words, make a sentence

✓ If you don't know one of the question words, head to the answer choices and rule out any that are not related and guess from what you have left

✓ On the last ten analogies, guess the weirdest answer choices

Strategy #1: Make a sentence from the question words

To use this strategy, you have to at least have a vague sense of what both question words mean. Basically, you make a sentence from the question words and then plug answer choices into that sentence to see which answer choice has the same relationship.

Here is an example:

1. Water is to ocean as
    (A) cloud is to sky
    (B) mountain is to hill
    (C) paint is to watercolor
    (D) ice is to glaciers
    (E) sneaker is to marathon

If we make a sentence from the question words, we might say "water makes up the ocean". Now we plug in our answer choices, subbing in the answer words for the question words. Does it make sense to say "cloud makes up the sky"? Sometimes that is true, but if we have to use the word sometimes, then it is not a strong relationship so we can rule out choice A. Does a "mountain make up a hill"? No, so choice B is gone. Does "paint make up a watercolor"? That doesn't make sense, so we can rule out choice C. Does "ice make up glaciers"? Yes. Choice D is correct. (We would keep going and plug in choice E just to make sure that it wasn't a better fit, but choice D is correct).

There are several relationships that show up frequently on the SSAT. If you become familiar with them, it makes it much easier to make up your own sentences quickly.

They are:

#1 Occupation- one word is the job of the other word
　　ex: Architect is to building

#2 Part of- one word is a part of the other word
　　ex: Kitchen is to house

#3 Type of- one word is a type of the other word, which is a broader category
  ex: Whale is to mammal

#4 Means without- one word means without the other word
  ex: Poor is to money

#5 Used for- one word is used to do the other word
  ex: Shovel is to dig

#6 Degree- the words have roughly the same meaning, only one is more extreme
  ex: Hungry is starving

#7 Characteristic of – one word is a characteristic of the other
  ex: Massive is to elephant

#8 Synonyms- the words are synonyms
  ex: Deceitful is to dishonest

#9 Antonyms- the words are opposite in meaning
  ex: Friendly is to rude

#10 Sequence- there is a distinct order that the words go in (months, time)
  ex: March is to July

#11 Found in- one word is found in the other
  ex: Shark is to ocean

And there is one final type of relationship. In some questions, the relationship will be between the first question word and the first answer word and the second question word and the second answer word. You may see one or two of these on the test (out of 30 analogy questions) so don't worry too much about them. Usually you will know the definition of the question words and you will know that they are not related.

#12 Weird ones – words that you know… and you know they aren't related

  ex: 1. Grass is to sky as
    (A) tree is to ground
    (B) green is to blue
    (C) boat is to ship
    (D) poem is to story
    (E) square is to circle

Choice B is correct. Grass is known for being green, and the sky is known for being blue. Don't let these questions throw you, just know that they are possibly out there.

Another type of "weird relationship" you might see is where the relationship has to do with how the words look. For example, the question might be "old is to mold". The relationship is that an m was added to the front of the word.

Strategy #2: If you don't know one of the question words, head to the answer choices and rule out any that are not related and guess from what you have left

If you read through the question words and don't know what one (or more!) of the question words mean, all is not lost. Sometimes there are answer choices with words that are not even related. Rule these out. Then plug the question words into the sentence you made from the remaining answer choices and see if it could work. Rule out any that don't. Guess from what you have left.

Keep in mind that if you find yourself using "could" "maybe, "can", or "sometimes", it is not a strong relationship so you should rule it out.

Here is an example:

1. (Weird word) is to ship as
   (A) luck is to delay
   (B) fun is to laughter
   (C) helmet is to football
   (D) mansion is to house
   (E) first is to last

Since we don't know one question word, we go to the answers. If we try to make a sentence from choice A, we can see that luck and delay just don't have a strong relationship. You could say that if you are lucky, you might not have a delay. However, that would be talking yourself into a relationship isn't strong at all (if you have to use sometimes, might, may, could, it is not a good relationship). Choice A is out. For choice B, you could say that laughter is the result of fun. However, if we plug the question words back into that sentence, is there anything that ship is a result of? Not really, so we can rule out choice B. If we look at choice C, you could say that that a helmet is worn to play football. But if we plug our question words into that sentence, is there anything that is worn to play ship? No. Choice C is out. On to choice D. A mansion is a type of house. Could something be a type of ship? Absolutely, so we keep choice D. Finally, choice E. First and last are opposites. But is there a word that means the opposite of ship? No, so choice E is out. We were able to narrow it down to one choice (choice D) without even knowing one of the question words.

Strategy #3: On the last ten analogies, guess the weirdest answer choices

The questions on this test go from easy to most difficult. Most students miss the last questions. However, most students REFUSE to guess words that they don't know. You know what this means, right? It means that if you want to raise your percentile score, you have to guess the answer choice that most students aren't going to guess.

Try to read through the answer choices in your head. The more difficulty you have pronouncing the words, the more likely it is to be the right answer choice on the last part of the analogies. This isn't an exact science, but it works often enough that you will come out ahead.

For example, let's say you guess the weirdest word on the last ten analogies and only get half of them correct. You get 5 points for the five that you got correct, and you only lose 1.25 points for the five that you missed. You come out ahead.

Those are the basic strategies for the synonyms and analogies. The other important piece of improving your verbal score is studying vocabulary. The workouts will help you with that, but you should also make flashcards for words that you run across that you do not know.

Reading Comprehension Section—Basic Strategies

The reading section consists of passages and questions. You can expect to see fiction, non-fiction, and poetry. The number of passages per test varies, but there tends to be 6-8 passages with 4-8 questions each. There will always be a total of 40 questions in the section, however.

The basic strategies for the reading comprehension section are:

- ✓ Before you read, go to the questions. If it is a general question (about the whole passage), mark it with a G. If it is a specific question, mark it with an S and then underline either the line reference or the key word of what it is asking about

- ✓ After you mark the questions, go ahead and read

- ✓ Answer specific questions first. If you can't underline the correct answer in the passage (reworded), then you haven't found it yet- keep looking!

- ✓ To answer general questions, reread the last sentence

Strategy #1: Before you read, mark the questions with a S or a G

It is important that you identify specific (S) and general (G) questions before you begin to read. You may come across the answer to a specific question as you read, so you also want to underline what the question is asking about for specific questions.

So how do you know if it is specific or general?

Here are some examples of the form that specific questions often take:

- ✓ In the first paragraph, the word _____ means

- ✓ In line 5, _____ means

- ✓ In line 7, _____ most likely refers to

- ✓ All of the following are mentioned EXCEPT

- ✓ All of the following questions are answered EXCEPT

If there is a line reference or the question has a lot of details in it, then it is probably a specific question.

If there is a line reference, go ahead and put a mark next to that line in the passage. That way you will know to go answer that question when you are reading. If the question asks about a specific detail, underline what it asks about so that you know what to look for when you read.

For example, let's say our question was:

1. How many years did it take Johnny Appleseed to plant his trees?

We would underline the word "years" since that is the detail we are looking for. Presumably, the whole passage would be about him planting trees so that would not be a helpful detail to look for.

Some questions may look general, but on the SSAT they are looking for a specific example.

Here is how these questions may look:

- ✓ The author would most likely agree

- ✓ Which of the following questions is answered by the passage?

- ✓ According to the passage/author

- ✓ It can be inferred from the passage

- ✓ This passage infers/implies which of the following

The reason that these questions are specific is that on the SSAT the answer to these question types will be found in a single sentence or two. In real life, that may not be true, but on this test, it is. We can't underline anything for these questions, however, since the details we are looking for are in the answer choices.

General questions ask about the passage as a whole.

They might look like:

- ✓ This passage primarily deals with

- ✓ This passage is mainly about

- ✓ The main purpose of this passage is to

- ✓ Which of the following best expresses the author's main point?

- ✓ What is the best title of this passage?

- ✓ The author's tone is

- ✓ The author's attitude is

If you see the words "main" or "primary" you have a general question on your hands and should mark it with a G.

Please keep in mind that you do not have to be correct every time when you mark S or G. Do not obsess over whether a question is specific or general. The point of this strategy is to save you time and it just isn't that big of a deal if you mark one question incorrectly.

Strategy #2: After you mark the questions, go ahead and read

As you read, keep an eye out for answers for specific questions. Don't read too slowly or feel like you need to memorize every sentence. If you come across a section that answers a question, then you slow down and read very, very carefully. There is no point in obsessing over material that there are no questions about, however.

Strategy #3: Answer specific questions first

The deal with specific questions is that you can find the answer restated in the passage. Always. If you haven't found it, then you just need to keep looking.

There are a few secrets to dealing with the specific reading questions.

They are:

Secret #1: Answers to specific questions are very detail oriented

Often the answer to questions can be found in just a word or two out of the whole passage. Also, the questions are not in order of the passage. The way to overcome this problem is to read the questions before reading the passage. That way, you know what you are looking for.

Secret #2: The test writers twist the words from the passage around so that the answer choice has the same words but a different meaning

For example, the passage may say that "John was upset when Sam got into the car with Trish."

The question may look something like:

1. Which of the following is implied by the author?
   (A) John was upset with Trish when Sam drove the car
   (B) John was upset with Trish when he got into the car
   (C) Sam and Trish were upset when John got into the car
   (D) John and Sam are cousins
   (E) John was not happy because Sam rode with Trish

Choices A, B, and C use words from the passage, but the order is switched around so that the meaning is different. Choice E restates what the passage says using different words that have the same meaning. That is what we are looking for.

To avoid making a mistake, watch out for answers that repeat exact words from the passage. Answers that repeat words aren't always wrong, but should be carefully analyzed the make sure that the meaning isn't twisted.

Secret #3: Our brain fills in words that simply are not there

As we read, we automatically fill in details.

For example, let's say that the passage says:

"Samuel came from a family of enormous height- it was said that even his mother was six feet four inches tall."

The question might then look like:

1. Which of the following about Samuel can be inferred from the passage?
   (A) That he is well educated
   (B) That he is very tall
   (C) His favorite pastime is basketball
   (D) He left school at an early age
   (E) He was the first astronaut to be a pet owner

As we read, our mind probably filled in that Samuel is tall since the passage says that his family was tall. However, the passage does NOT say that Samuel is tall. Odds are good that we won't remember this, however, since our mind has already filled in the blank. We would choose choice B, even though it is incorrect.

The way that we overcome this is by underlining the evidence in the passage for the correct answer choice for specific questions. Every. Single. Time. If you can't underline the answer, you just haven't found it yet.

If you remember to apply these secrets, you should ace the specific questions.

Strategy #4: Before answering general questions, reread the last sentence of the entire passage

On the SSAT, you want to answer general questions last. The reason we do this is that by the time that you have answered all of the specific questions, you generally have read the passage several times.

One hazard of having looked at all the details of a passage closely is that we sometimes lose sight of the main idea. If we reread the last sentence before answering general questions, it will keep us focused on the main idea.

Often, several of the answer choices for general questions will be a detail from the passage. You might be able to find evidence for that answer in the passage, but it will be wrong because this is a general question and NOT a specific one! Look for the answer choice that comes closest in meaning to the very last sentence of the entire passage.

Now that you have the strategies, it is time to head to the workouts!

The format of each workout is very predictable so that you can focus on the material and not the directions. Here is what you should look for:

- ✓ **First there is a vocabulary section. Each vocabulary section has:**

  - Roots and words that have those roots. Be sure to memorize the roots because there will be different words in later workouts that have those same roots

  - Words to remember. These are words that you just need to memorize

- ✓ **Practice for the verbal section**

  - At first, the focus will be more on strategy than content. Be patient and work through it. We want the strategy to become automatic so that you don't even have to think about it on test day. Think of this part as being like soccer drills. Not always fun, but totally necessary for game day

- ✓ **Practice for the reading section**

  - We will start out with working on identifying specific and general questions, then there will be one reading passage in each workout

- ✓ **Math practice**

  - The focus here is to get through as much of the content as possible. Be sure to understand why you missed questions before moving on to the next workout

You may notice that in workouts #2 and #3, there are blanks in the strategy summaries for you to fill in. Please do NOT skip this section. The goal of this book is to make success automatic, so we have to practice. Gradually, the workouts will transition from telling you all of the strategies beforehand to having you complete a checklist after you are done.

There is a method to this madness- the repetition will make the strategies stick even when there is stress on test day.

Also, make flashcards for words that you do not know and practice them frequently! Seriously, take them in the car, to study hall, and everywhere else that you go.

Go get 'em!

Workout #1

Verbal Section

Vocab

Below are some roots. I will give you the definition of the root and then two examples of words that have that root. Look up the meaning of those words and write the definitions in the blanks provided. As you look up the definition of each word, think about how it relates to the root. After you write the definition of each word, write a sentence using the word or a memory trick or association for remembering the word.

Root: de – the opposite of or away from
Deter-
Definition:

Sentence or memory trick:

Descent-
Definition:

Sentence or memory trick:

Root: cis – to cut
Excise-
Definition:

Sentence or memory trick:

Concise-
Defintion:

Sentence or memory trick:

Frugal- adjective describing someone who doesn't like to spend money
Ex: My mother says she is frugal, but I say she is cheap!

Now, MAKE FLASHCARDS FOR ALL THE WORDS ABOVE- AND STUDY THEM!

Synonyms strategy review

If you know the word, think of a definition before you look at answer choices.

If you have heard the word but can't define it:

1) Use context- in what sentence or phrase have you heard the word before?

2) Positive or negative- write a plus or minus sign next to the question word, rule out answer choices that are opposite or neutral

3) Look for roots and word parts- ask yourself what other words this word looks like

Synonyms practice. Before you answer the question, I want you to write beside it which strategy you used from above.

1. INCISION: *Strategy:*
    (A) smile
    (B) mockery
    (C) accident
    (D) cut
    (E) excuse

2. THRIFTY: *Strategy:*
    (A) swift
    (B) frugal
    (C) mean
    (D) stubborn
    (E) frumpy

3. DETOUR: *Strategy:*
    (A) roundabout path
    (B) needle
    (C) fulcrum
    (D) center
    (E) road

Analogies Strategy Review

1) If you know the question words, make a sentence from them

2) If you don't know the question words, go to the answer choices and:

   A) Try to make a sentence with the answer choices. Rule out any answer choices where there is not a strong relationship between the two words. If you hear yourself using the words "can, maybe, could, sometimes", you are talking yourself into the wrong answer

   B) With the choices left, try to plug the question words into the sentence that you made with the answer choice words. Could it work?

3) If you are stuck on the last ten analogies, simply pick the answer choice with the weirdest word

4) Keep in mind that there are weird ones. You will know it is a weird one because you will know the meaning of both question words and they will not be related

Analogies Practice

Listed below are some of the common relationships used on this test:

#1 Occupation- one word is the job of the other word

#2 Part of- one word is a part of the other word

#3 Type of- one word is a type of the other word, which is a broader category

#4 Means without- one word means without the other word

#5 Used for- one word is used to do the other word

#6 Degree- the words have roughly the same meaning, only one is more extreme

#7 Characteristic of – one word is a characteristic of the other

#8 Synonyms- the words have the same meaning

#9 Antonyms- the words are opposite in meaning

#10 Sequence- there is a distinct order that the words go in (months, time)

#11 Found in- one word is found in the other

#12 Weird ones – words that you know... and you know they aren't related

Below are sample analogies. Write the number of the relationship from above that they use.

1. Drought is to rain as   *Relationship #_____*

2. Elbow is arm as   *Relationship #_____*

3. Scythe is to cut as   *Relationship #_____*

4. Miffed is to irate as   *Relationship #_____*

5. Frugal is to cheapskate as   *Relationship #_____*

6. March is to June as   *Relationship #_____*

7. Concise is to wordy as   *Relationship #_____*

8. Shoe is to coat as   *Relationship #_____*

9. Snake is to reptile as   *Relationship #_____*

10. Monkey is to jungle as   *Relationship #_____*

Reading Section

Reading Strategies

The first step when you approach each passage is to look at the questions first. You will want to label each question with either an S or a G. If it is a specific question, label it with an S. If it is a general question, label it with a G.

Then read the passage. Answer specific questions as you go. Answer general questions at the end.

Tricks for answering specific questions:

1) You can almost always underline the correct answer in the passage for these questions. If you can't underline your answer (often restated using synonyms), then you haven't found the right answer- keep looking!

2) The wrong answer choices often take the same words from the passage and then twist around the order so that they have a different meaning

3) Look out for assumptions that you make that are not backed up by the passage

Tricks for general questions:

1) They often have the words mainly or primarily in them

2) Before answering these questions, reread the last sentence of the entire passage

3) The wrong answers are often mentioned in the passage, but they are details and NOT the main idea

Reading Practice

Label the following with a G or S: (G is for general, S is for specific)

1) This passage is primarily about

2) According to the passage, all of the following are rituals of the Navajo EXCEPT

3) The purpose of this document was to

4) The passage implies that the secession of Southern states happened in the year

5) In this poem, the path represents which of the following

Math Section

Math Strategies

Our general strategies include:

1) Use estimating- this is a multiple choice test!

2) If there are variables in the answer choices, try plugging in your own numbers. If it is a "must be true" question, try plugging in weird numbers such as negatives, zero, and fractions

3) If they ask for the value of a variable, plug in answer choices

4) If you can, find a range that the answer should fall within

Math Practice Section

1. There are 25 students in a class. 18 of these students play the piano. 9 of these students play the trombone. How many students must play both the piano and the trombone?
    - (A) 1
    - (B) 2
    - (C) 3
    - (D) 9
    - (E) 25

Questions 2-3 refer to the following definition.

For all real numbers q and r, $q \# r = (q+r) \times (q-r)$

Example: $2 \# 3 = (2+3) \times (2-3) = 5 \times -1 = -5$

2. $5 \# 4 =$
    - (A) 6
    - (B) 7
    - (C) 8
    - (D) 9
    - (E) 10

3. If $T \# 2 = 77$, then $T =$
    - (A) 3
    - (B) 5
    - (C) 9
    - (D) 11
    - (E) 20

4. Sarah has y baseball cards. She has seven more cards than Tim. Tim has four less cards than Sheila. In terms of y, how many baseball cards does Sheila have?
    - (A) $y - 3$
    - (B) $y - 7$
    - (C) $y - 10$
    - (D) $y + 4$
    - (E) $y + 10$

5. John is laying a brick patio. His bricks are 3 inches by 4 inches. The patio he wants to create will be five feet by five feet. How many bricks will he need?
    (A) 12
    (B) 25
    (C) 60
    (D) 150
    (E) 300

Workout #1 Answers

Vocabulary- I am not giving you answers for the definitions- look them up!

Synonyms Practice

1. D- the word incision has the "cis" root, which means to cut

2. B- thrifty and frugal are two words that you just have to memorize. Be sure to make flashcards if you missed this one

3. A- de means opposite or away from. A detour takes you away from something, so it is a roundabout path. Don't be fooled by choice E. Detours are often on roads, but detour and road don't mean the same thing.

Analogies Practice

1. #4- drought means without rain

2. #2 or #5- an elbow is part of the arm or an elbow is used for bending the arm. You would just have to go through the answer choices to see which relationship they were looking for

3. #5- a scythe is used to cut

4. #6- miffed is a little angry, irate is really, really angry

5. #7- frugal is a characteristic of a cheapskate

6. #10- there are two months between Match and June

7. #9- concise and wordy have opposite meanings

8. #12- these are both easy words and we know they aren't related, so it must be a weird one

9. #3- a snake is a type of reptile

10. #11- a monkey is found in the jungle

Reading Practice:

1. G- the word "primarily" tells us that it is general

2. S- this is looking for details

3. G- the question is referring to the document as a whole so it is general

4. S- questions that use "implies" are almost always specific on the SSAT

5. S or G- it is probably specific, but it is possible that the whole poem was about the path. Remember, we don't obsess over being exact when we label questions S or G. Sometimes we just have to go with it and see how the passage plays out.

Math Practice:

1. B- If we add 18+9, then we get 27. However, there are only 25 students. This tells us that there must be an overlap of 2 students that play both instruments.

2. D- Don't worry if you were confused about what the # sign meant. You aren't supposed to know. This is a particular type of SSAT question where they define a function for you and then you have to plug in. For this question, the 5 comes before the # sign, so we plug in 5 for q in the equation. The 3 comes after the # sign, so plug in the 3 for the r in the equation.

   We get:

   $$(5 + 4) \times (5 - 4) = 9 \times 1 = 9$$

3. C – We use the same equation as we did for #2. Only this time we have to plug in a variable.

   If we plug in, we get:

   $$(T + 2) \times (T - 2) = 77$$

   We could solve the math way, but that could get tricky and we might make a mistake. It would be better just to plug in the answer choices for T and see what works. If we try choice C, we get:

   $$(9 + 2) \times (9 - 2) = 11 \times 7 = 77$$

Since we got 77 for our answer, choice C is correct

4. A- We have variables in the answer choices, so we plug in our own numbers. Let's make $y=10$, so Sarah has 10 baseball cards. She has seven more than Tim, so Tim must have 3 cards. Tim has four less cards than Sheila, so Sheila must have 7 cards. We circle 7 since we were looking for how many cards Sheila has. Now we plug in 10 for y in the answer choices and see what gives us 7.

    (A) $y - 3 = 10 - 3 = 7$
    (B) $y - 7 = 10 - 7 = 3$
    (C) $y - 10 = 10 - 10 = 0$
    (D) $y + 4 = 10 + 4 = 14$
    (E) $y + 10 = 10 + 10 = 20$

    Since we got 7 for choice A, and 7 was our target, choice A is the correct answer.

5. E – The first thing that you should notice is that there are both inches and feet as units of measurement in this problem. We need to make sure not to get tripped up by that. The first step is to convert all of the measurements into inches. In order to do that, we multiply 5 feet by 12 to get 60 inches. That tells us that the patio is going to be 60 inches by 60 inches. Let's assume that he lays all the bricks going the same direction. If we divide 60 by 3 (since one side of the bricks is 3 inches), we get that he can fit 20 bricks on one side. To see how many bricks fit in the other dimension, we divide 60 by 4 (since the other side of the bricks is 4 inches) and get 15. That tells us that the patio will be 20 bricks by 15 bricks, or twenty rows of 15 bricks each. If we multiply 15 times 20, we get that he needs a total of 300 bricks, or answer choice E.

Workout #2

Verbal Section

Vocab

Below are some roots. I will give you the definition of the root and then two examples of words that have that root. Look up the meaning of those words and write the definitions in the blanks provided. As you look up the definition of each word, think about how it relates to the root. After you write the definition of each word, write a sentence using the word or a memory trick or association for remembering the word.

Root: fid- trust or faith
Fidelity-
Definition:

Sentence or memory trick:

Infidel-
Definition:

Sentence or memory trick:

Root: pan- all
Panorama-
Definition:

Sentence or memory trick:

Panacea-
Definition:

Sentence or memory trick:

Word to Remember!!!

Congeal- to thicken or become a solid from a liquid
Ex: It is nasty how the fat from French fries congeals when they get cold.

Now, MAKE FLASHCARDS FOR ALL THE WORDS ABOVE- AND STUDY THEM!

Synonyms strategy review

Fill in the blanks

If you know the word, think of a definition before you look at answer choices

If you have heard the word but can't define it:

1) Use context- _____
   _____?

2) Positive or negative- write a _____next to the question word,
   rule out answer choices that are opposite or _____

3) Look for roots and word parts- _____
   _____

Synonyms practice

Before you answer the question, I want you to write beside it which strategy you used
from above.

1. DECELERATE: *Strategy:*
   (A) speed up
   (B) turn around
   (C) fall
   (D) stumble
   (E) slow down

2. CONGEAL: *Strategy:*
   (A) smell
   (B) let loose
   (C) curdle
   (D) resist
   (E) rise

3. TREACHERY: *Strategy:*
    (A)   event
    (B)   perfidy
    (C)   salvation
    (D)   eulogy
    (E)   crowd

Analogies Strategy Review

Fill in the blanks

1) If you know the question words, _____.

2) If you don't know the question words, _____and:

    A) Try to make a sentence with the answer choices. Rule out any that do not have a strong relationship. If you hear yourself using the words "_____ _____", you are talking yourself into the wrong answer

    B) With the choices left, _____ _____into the sentence that you made with the answer choice words. Could it work?

3) If you are stuck on the last ten analogies, simply pick the answer choice with the _____.

4) Keep in mind that there are weird ones. You will know it is a weird one because you will know the meaning of both question words and _____ _____.

Analogies Practice

Listed below are some of the common relationships used on this test:

#1 Occupation- one word is the job of the other word

#2 Part of- one word is a part of the other word

#3 Type- one word is a type of the other word, which is a broader category

#4 Means without- one word means without the other word

#5 Used for- one word is used to do the other word

#6 Degree- the words have roughly the same meaning, only one is more extreme

#7 Characteristic of – one word is a characteristic of the other

#8 Synonyms- the words have the same meaning

9 Antonyms- the words are opposite in meaning

#10 Sequence- there is a distinct order that the words go in (months, time)

#11 Found in- one word is found in the other

#12 Weird ones – words that you know... and you know they aren't related

Below are sample analogies. Write the number of the relationship from above that they use.

1.   Policeman is to law enforcement as   *Relationship #_____*

2.   Magnanimous is to malevolent as   *Relationship #_____*

3.   Buckle is to belt as   *Relationship #_____*

4.   Pencil is to writing as   *Relationship #_____*

5.   Soccer is to tennis as   *Relationship #_____*

6.   Poverty is to wealth as   *Relationship #_____*

7.   Compass is to navigation as   *Relationship #_____*

8.   Rivulet is to river as   *Relationship #_____*

9.   Diamond is to mine as   *Relationship #_____*

10.   Nimble is to gymnast as   *Relationship #_____*

Reading Section

Reading Strategies

Fill in the blank

The first step when you approach each passage is to_____. You will want to label each question with either an_____. If it is a specific question, label it with an __. If it is a general question, label it with a __.

Then read the passage. Answer _____ questions as you go. Answer _____ questions at the end.

Tricks for answering specific questions:

1) You can almost always underline the correct answer in the passage for these questions. If you can't _____ your answer (often restated using synonyms), _____- keep looking!

2) The wrong answer choices often take the same words from the passage and then _____.

3) Look out for assumptions that you make that are not _____ _____.

Tricks for general questions:

1) They often have the words _____ in them

2) Before answering these questions, reread the _____ of the entire passage

3) The wrong answers are often mentioned in the passage, but they _____ _____.

Reading Practice

Label the following with a G or S: (G is for general, S is for specific)

1) An appropriate title for this poem would be

2) According to this passage, Johnny Appleseed

3) The author implies that suffragettes

4) The author's attitude toward early veterinarians can best be described as

5) The author uses the analogy of willows to illustrate that Native Americans

Math Strategies

Fill in the blank

Our general strategies include:

1) Use _____ - this is a multiple choice test!

2) If there are variables in the answer choices, try _____.
   If it is a "must be true" question, try plugging in weird numbers such as negatives, zero, and fractions

3) If they ask for the value of a variable, _____

4) If you can, _____ that the answer should fall within

Math Practice Section

1) The glee club was having a flower sale. At 10 AM, they needed to sell five more flowers to reach their goal. By 1 PM, they had exceeded their goal by 12 flowers. How many flowers did they sell between 10 AM and 1 PM?
   (A) 5
   (B) 7
   (C) 10
   (D) 15
   (E) 17

2. If $\frac{1}{3}Q = 9$, then $\frac{2}{3}Q =$
   (A) 3
   (B) 9
   (C) 12
   (D) 18
   (E) 27

3. When two triangular regions overlap, which of the following shapes could describe the overlapping portion?
   I.   Triangle
   II.   Square
   III. Rectangle

   (A) I only
   (B) II only
   (C) I and III only
   (D) I, II, and III
   (E) None of the above

4. 25 % of $11.95 is closest to which of the following
   (A) $3.00
   (B) $4.00
   (C) $6.00
   (D) $8.00
   (E) $12.00

5. If the average of 5 consecutive odd numbers is 13, what is the smallest number?
   (A) 7
   (B) 9
   (C) 11
   (D) 13
   (E) 17

Workout #2 Answers

Vocabulary- Look them up!

Synonyms strategy review:

... in what sentence or phrase have you heard the word before?

...plus or minus sign.. neutral

...ask yourself what other word this word looks like

Synonyms practice:

1. E – the de root means opposite. If accelerate means to speed up, then decelerate would be the opposite, or to slow down

2. C- this was a word to remember. Make sure you make a flashcard if you missed this one!

3. B- treachery is an act of betrayal. Perfidy has the fid root that means faithful. Perfidy means a betrayal of trust, so it is the correct answer. If nothing else, you could have ruled out some choices and then guessed (by the way, a eulogy is a speech of praise)

Analogies strategy review:

...make a sentence from them

...go to the answer choices

...can, maybe, could, sometimes

...try to plug in the question words

...weirdest word

...they will not be related

Analogies Practice:

1. #1- the job of a policeman is law enforcement

2. #9- magnanimous is generous and giving, malevolent is wishing evil to others

3. #2 or #5- a buckle is part of a belt or a buckle is used to close a belt

4. #5- a pencil is used for writing

5. #12- soccer and tennis seem to go together, but are not actually related. On this test, if two things are both part of the same broader category (sports in this case), that is not a relationship that works

6. #4- poverty means without wealth

7. #5- a compass is used for navigation

8. #6- a rivulet is like a really little river

9. #11- a diamond is found in a mine

10. #7- nimble is a characteristic of a gymnast

Reading Strategies

...look at the questions first

...S or G

...S...G

...specific...general

...underline...you haven't found the right answer

...twist around the order so that they mean something else

...backed up by the passage

...mainly and primarily

...the last sentence

...are details and NOT the main idea

Reading Practice:

1. G- a title has to sum up the passage as a whole, so it is a general question

2. S- even though it looks general, on the SSAT "according to the passage" questions are almost always looking for a detail

3. S – Because we know how the SSAT generally works, we know that "implies" questions are usually looking for a detail

4. S or G- Depends on whether or not the whole passage is about early veterinarians. I would guess that the question is specific since it uses the qualifier "early". You would have to make sure you chose the answer that summed up the author's attitude about "early veterinarians" and not just veterinarians in general

5. S- an analogy is usually a small part of a passage and not the entire thing.

Math strategies:

...estimating...

...plugging in your own numbers...

...plug in answer choices...

...find a range...

1. E- To solve this problem, let's plug in our own number for their goal. Let's say they wanted to sell 10 flowers. So at 10 AM they would have sold 5. flowers. By 1 PM, they would have sold 22 flowers. If I find the difference between these two numbers, I get that they sold 17 flowers in between

2. D- $\frac{2}{3}$ is twice as much as $\frac{1}{3}$. That means that the value of $\frac{2}{3}Q$ should be twice the value of $\frac{1}{3}Q$. Twice the value of 9 is 18, so choice D is my answer.

3. D- Draw this one out. If one tip of one triangle overlapped with the other, a triangle would be created. Since it doesn't tell us that triangles can't be right triangles, we have to assume that is a possibility. If we have two right triangles, and the right angles overlapped, then we could create both a square and a rectangle. Therefore, I, II, and III all work.

4. A- We can round off since it uses the words "closest to". $11.95 is about $12.00, so we can use that number for calculations. Now we can use the trick of finding 10% and then using that to find 25%. To get 10%, we can just move the decimal place one place to the left, so we get 1.20

Here is how we figure out 25% from that:

```
10%=1.20
10%=1.20
+ 5%=0.60
-----------------
25%=3.00
```

5. B- The trick to this problem is remembering that it is consecutive ODD numbers and that they are looking for the SMALLEST number. I would circle these two facts in the problem because they are easy to forget. If the numbers are consecutive, then the average is also the middle number. That means there must be two numbers before 13, so we can count backwards by two. If the third number is thirteen, then the second number must be 11, so the first number must be 9. The smallest number is 9, so choice B is correct.

Workout #3

Verbal Section

Vocab

Below are some roots. I will give you the definition of the root and then two examples of words that have that root. Look up the meaning of those words and write the definitions in the blanks provided. As you look up the definition of each word, think about how it relates to the root. After you write the definition of each word, write a sentence using the word or a memory trick or association for remembering the word.

Root: loc/loq/log- to speak
Eloquent-
Definition:

Sentence or memory trick:

Neologism-
Definition:

Sentence or memory trick:

Root: magna- big
Magnanimous-
Definition:

Sentence or memory trick:

Magnificent-
Definition:

Sentence or memory trick:

Word to Remember!!!

Tact- words or actions designed not to offend another person (A person with tact is tactful)

Ex: You have to show a certain amount of tact when telling someone he has a booger on his face.

Now, MAKE FLASHCARDS FOR ALL THE WORDS ABOVE- AND STUDY THEM!

Synonyms strategy review

If you know the word, think of a definition before you look at answer choices

If you have heard the word but can't define it:

1) Use _____- in what sentence or phrase have you heard the word before?

2) _____- write a plus or minus sign next to the question word, rule out answer choices that are opposite or neutral

3) _____- ask yourself what other words this word looks like

Synonyms practice.

Before you answer the question, I want you to write beside it which strategy you used from above.

1.   LOQUACIOUS: *Strategy:*
     (A)   jubilant
     (B)   fussy
     (C)   fundamental
     (D)   profound
     (E)   talkative

2.   GENEROUS: *Strategy:*
     (A)   magnanimous
     (B)   funky
     (C)   klutzy
     (D)   gifted
     (E)   slow

3. DERIDE: *Strategy:*
    (A) elevate
    (B) obsess
    (C) ruin
    (D) ridicule
    (E) chase

Analogies Strategy Review

1) If_____, make a sentence
    from them.

2) If_____, go to the
    answer choices and:

    A) _____with the answer choices. Rule
        out any that do not have a strong relationship. If you hear yourself using the
        words "can, maybe, could, sometimes", you are _____
        _____

    B) _____, try to plug the question
        words into the sentence that you made with the answer choice words. Could
        it work?

3) _____
    _____, simply pick the answer choice with the weirdest word.

4) Keep in mind that there are_____. You will know it is a
    _____ because you will know the meaning of both ques-
    tion words and they will not be related.

Analogies Practice

Now that you are more familiar with the relationships, pretend the following are answer
choices when you don't know the question words. Rule out the ones that are not related.
Remember, if you use can, could, maybe, or sometimes, it is not a strong relationship!

1. clown is to tiger

2. shoe is to foot

3. sour is to sweet

4. perimeter is to circle

5. frugal is to spendthrift

6. corral is to horses

7. morning is to tired

8. overcast is to sunshine

Reading Section

Reading Strategies

The first step when you approach each passage is to_____.
You will want to label each question with either an S or a G. If it is a _____
question, label it with an S. If it is a _____ question, label it with a G.

Then read the passage. Answer _____ questions as you go. Answer
_____ questions at the end.

Tricks for answering specific questions:

1) You can almost always underline the correct answer in the passage for these questions. If you can't underline your answer (often_____),
   then you haven't found the right answer- _____!

2) The wrong answer choices often take the same words from the passage and then
   _____.

3) Look out for assumptions that you make that are not _____
   _____.

Tricks for general questions:

1) They often have the words _____in them

2) Before answering these questions, reread the _____ of the entire
   passage.

3) The wrong answers are_____,
   but they are details and NOT the main idea

Reading Practice

Label the following with a G or S: (G is for general, S is for specific)

1. The Battle of Midway was fought

2. Which of the following best expresses the author's main point

3. The passage implies

4. The tone of the passage can best be described as

5. Which of the following statements about exports would the author most likely agree with

Math Strategies

Fill in the blank

Our general strategies include:

1) Use _____ - this is a multiple choice test!

2) If there are variables in the answer choices, try _____.
   If it is a "must be true" question, try plugging in weird numbers such as negatives, zero, and fractions

3) If they ask for the value of a variable, _____

4) If you can, _____that the answer should fall within

Math Practice Section

1. How the Smiths spent their $200 road trip budget

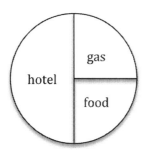

Figure 1

According to the graph in figure 1, how much did the Smith family spend on gas for their road trip?

(A) $25
(B) $50
(C) $75
(D) $100
(E) $150

2. For a bake sale, the track team sold cookies and doughnuts. They sold twice as many cookies as doughnuts. Which of the following could have been the total number of cookies and doughnuts sold?

(A) 10
(B) 14
(C) 16
(D) 21
(E) 25

3. A three man team competed in a relay race. Each person completed one leg of the race. If the average time per leg was 3 minutes and 35 seconds, what was the total time it took the team to complete the race?

(A) 9 minutes and 35 seconds
(B) 10 minutes and 15 seconds
(C) 10 minutes and 45 seconds
(D) 11 minutes
(E) 11 minutes and 35 seconds

4. Farmer Bill must put up a new fence around his hog pen. He needs the total perimeter to be 12 yards. If the fence comes in segments 2 feet long, how many segments will he need?

(A) 3
(B) 4
(C) 6
(D) 12
(E) 18

5. Five friends each chip in 7 dollars for a present. If 2 more people chipped in for the same present, and the expense was shared equally, how much less would each person have to pay?
    (A) $2
    (B) $3
    (C) $5
    (D) $7
    (E) $35

Workout #3 Answers

Vocabulary- Look them up!

Synonyms strategy review

...context...

...positive or negative...

...Look for roots and word parts...

Synonyms practice:

1. E- loquacious has the loq root, which means to speak. A loquacious person is talkative.

2. A- magna means big, and the anim root means spirit, so if you are magnanimous you have a big spirit, or are generous

3. D- de is a negative root, so we know the answer must be negative. Ruin and ridicule are both negative. However, do you notice that deride and ridicule both have rid in them? To deride someone is to ridicule (or criticize) him.

Analogies strategy review:

...you know the words...

...you don't know the question words...

...Try to make a sentence... talking yourself into the wrong answer choice

...With the choices left...

...If you are stuck on the last ten analogies...

...weird ones... weird one...

Analogies practice:

The following are NOT related: 1, 4, 7

For #1, a clown and a tiger might both show up in the circus, but that is not a strong relationship. Remember, on this test belonging to the same broader category (circus performers) doesn't count as a relationship.

For #4, it is tempting to say they are related because they are both geometry terms. However, a circle has a circumference, not a perimeter

For #7, you may be tired in the morning, but you may not be tired at all. If you have to use the word may, the relationship is not strong enough

Reading strategies:

...look at the questions first...specific...general

...specific...general

..restated using synonyms...keep looking!

...twist around the order so that they have a different meaning

...supported by the passage

...primarily and mainly

...very last sentence of the passage

...often mentioned in the passage

Reading practice:

1. S

2. G

3. S- Even though it looks general, these questions are almost always looking for a detail

4. G

5. S- Again, these questions generally are not about the main idea, but rather a detail

Math Strategies:

...estimating...

...plugging in your own numbers...

...plug in answer choices...

...find a range...

1. B- the Smiths spent about a quarter of their budget on gas. Their total budget was $200, and if we divide $200 into four pieces, or quarters, then we get $50 spent on gas

2. D- the ratio of cookies to doughnuts was 2 to 1. If we convert these ratios into fractions, we get that 1/3 of their sales were doughnuts and 2/3 were cookies. This tells us that the total number of items sold must be divisible by 3. Answer choice D is the only one divisible by 3

3. C- if we rearrange the average equation, we get that average X number of numbers = total. This tells us that we should multiply 3 minutes and 35 second by three. This gives us ten minutes and 45 seconds

4. E- we have both feet and yards in this problem. Our first step is to convert the yards into feet. To do this, we multiply 12 times 3 to get 36 feet around the hog pen. We can then divide this number by 2 since each segment is 2 feet long. We get that the farmer will need 18 segments

5. A- if we multiply 5 X 7, that tells us that $35 was collected originally. If two more people gave money, then there would now be 7 people giving money. Since the total amount of money collected did not change, we divide $35 by 7 to get that each person now gives $5. This is $2 less than the original $7 a piece, so choice A is correct

Workout #4

Verbal Section

Vocab

Below are some roots. I will give you the definition of the root and then two examples of words that have that root. Look up the meaning of those words and write the definitions in the blanks provided. As you look up the definition of each word, think about how it relates to the root. After you write the definition of each word, write a sentence using the word or a memory trick or association for remembering the word.

Root: bene- good or well
Beneficient
Definition:

Sentence or memory trick:

Benefactor-
Definition:

Sentence or memory trick:

Root: chron- time
Chronic-
Definition:

Sentence or memory trick:

Anachronism-
Definition:

Sentence or memory trick:

Word to Remember!!!

Scull- A boat used for rowing
Ex: In the fall, you can often see sculls cruising along the Charles River

Now, MAKE FLASHCARDS FOR ALL THE WORDS ABOVE- AND STUDY THEM!

Synonyms strategy review

If you know the word, think of a definition before you look at answer choices

If you have heard the word but can't define it:

1) Use context- in what sentence or phrase have you heard the word before?

2) Positive or negative- write a plus or minus sign next to the question word, rule out answer choices that are opposite or neutral

3) Look for roots and word parts- ask yourself what other words this word looks like

Synonyms practice.

Before you answer the question, I want you to write beside it which strategy you used from above.

TIME YOURSELF- THESE QUESTIONS SHOULD TAKE LESS THAN 3 MINUTES.

1. BENEDICTION: *Strategy:*
   (A) meeting
   (B) accident
   (C) ruse
   (D) blessing
   (E) race

2. RECURRING: *Strategy:*
   (A) last
   (B) chronic
   (C) symbolic
   (D) rusty
   (E) fast paced

3. DEVALUE: *Strategy:*
   (A) debase
   (B) increase
   (C) end
   (D) meditate
   (E) guess

4. LOQUACIOUS: *Strategy:*
   (A) mundane
   (B) rowdy
   (C) moist
   (D) extinct
   (E) talkative

5. DIPLOMATIC   *Strategy:*
   (A) rough
   (B) flawed
   (C) tactful
   (D) growing
   (E) sharp

Analogies Strategy Review

1) If you know the question words, make a sentence from them.

2) If you don't know the question words, go to the answer choices and:

   A) Try to make a sentence with the answer choices. Rule out any that do not have a strong relationship. If you hear yourself using the words "can, maybe, could, sometimes", you are talking yourself into the wrong answer

   B) With the choices left, try to plug the question words into the sentence that you made with the answer choice words. Could it work?

3) If you are stuck on the last ten analogies, simply pick the answer choice with the weirdest word.

4) Keep in mind that there are weird ones. You will know it is a weird one because you will know the meaning of both question words and they will not be related.

Analogies Practice

Listed below are some of the common relationships used on this test:

#1 Occupation- one word is the job of the other word

#2 Part of- one word is a part of the other word

#3 Type of- one word is a type of the other word, which is a broader category

#4 Means without- one word means without the other word

#5 Used for- one word is used to do the other word

#6 Degree- the words have roughly the same meaning, only one is more extreme

#7 Characteristic of – one word is a characteristic of the other

#8 Synonyms- the words have the same meaning

9 Antonyms- the words are opposite in meaning

#10 Sequence- there is a distinct order that the words go in (months, time)

#11 Found in- one word is found in the other

#12 Weird ones – words that you know... and you know they aren't related

Below are sample analogy questions.

Next to each question:

(A)   If you know the question words, write in the relationship number from the list above.

(B)   If you don't know the question words, write in WB (for working backwards)

TIME YOURSELF- THESE QUESTIONS SHOULD TAKE LESS THAN 3 MINUTES.

1.   Panacea is to cure as   *Relationship #/Strategy:*
     (A)   vacuum is to clean
     (B)   medicine is to infect
     (C)   butcher is to carve
     (D)   water is to pour
     (E)   hindrance is to enjoy

2. Magnificent is to miniscule   *Relationship #/ Strategy:*
   (A)   tremendous is to noisy
   (B)   superficial is to shallow
   (C)   abstract is to concrete
   (D)   generous is to benevolent
   (E)   fundamental is to worrisome

3. Infidelity is to betrayal as   *Relationship #/ Strategy:*
   (A)   peace is to riot
   (B)   clown is to performer
   (C)   hammer is to carpenter
   (D)   force is to bravery
   (E)   luck is to wealth

4. Excise is to eradicate   *Relationship #/Strategy:*
   (A)   chronicle is to record
   (B)   recede is to storm
   (C)   ignite is to resist
   (D)   write is to listen
   (E)   deter is to forbid

5. Jot is to tot   *Relationship #/Strategy:*
   (A)   write is to compose
   (B)   mold is to cold
   (C)   junk is to trunk
   (D)   run is to jog
   (E)   fast is to slow

Reading Section

Reading Strategies

The first step when you approach each passage is to look at the questions first. You will want to label each question with either an S or a G. If it is a specific question, label it with an S. If it is a general question, label it with a G.

Then read the passage. Answer specific questions as you go. Answer general questions at the end.

Tricks for answering specific questions:

1) You can almost always underline the correct answer in the passage for specific questions. If you can't underline your answer (often restated using synonyms), then you haven't found the right answer- keep looking!

2) The wrong answer choices often take the same words from the passage and then twist around the order so that they have a different meaning.

3) Look out for assumptions that you make that are not backed up by the passage

Tricks for general questions:

1) They often have the words mainly or primarily in them

2) Before answering these questions, reread the last sentence of the entire passage

3) The wrong answers are often mentioned in the passage, but they are details and NOT the main idea

Reading Practice

Below is a practice reading passage. It is a science passage, one of the many types that you will see on this test.

TIME YOURSELF- THIS PASSAGE AND QUESTIONS SHOULD TAKE A TOTAL OF 5 MINUTES

If you look into the night sky, you may notice something that looks like a very bright star. It might, in fact, be Venus. The moon is the brightest object in the night sky, but Venus ranks second. Venus is also the second planet from the sun.

Venus has been nicknamed Earth's "sister planet" because it is similar to Earth in size, gravity, and composition. It is even believed that at one time, Venus may have possessed oceans, just like those on Earth. However, these oceans evaporated long ago leaving just a dry and dusty surface covered with volcanoes.

Volcanoes are one of the most prominent features of Venus' geography. There is a large amount of sulfur in Venus' atmosphere, which indicates that these volcanoes have been active some time in recent history. However, there is no evidence of lava, which leaves scientists puzzled. Volcanoes or volcanic activity caused many of the surface features on Venus.

Venus has long fascinated people in many cultures. It is often called either the "morning star" or the "evening star". Depending upon where Earth and

Venus are in their relative rotations around the sun, it can appear to either be the last star on the horizon in the morning or the first star in evening. Pythagoras is often given credit for discovering that these two stars were actually the same body some time in the sixth century, B.C. We now know, of course, that these are not stars at all, but rather the planet Venus.

Venus remained relatively unknown until the twentieth century. After a few unfruitful attempts, in 1966 the unmanned probe Venera 3 crashed into the surface of Venus. Unfortunately, its equipment was damaged and it was unable to send information back to Earth. The Venera 4, however, was able to safely land on Venus and communicate data back to scientists. Since then, other probes have provided us with further information about Earth's "sister planet".

1. The author states that Venus has been called Earth's "sister planet" because
    (A) It is believed that Venus spun off of Earth
    (B) It is similar in color to Earth
    (C) It has oceans like Earth does
    (D) Early scientists thought that it rotated around Earth
    (E) It is about the same size as Earth and made up of a similar composition

2. Which of the following can currently be found on Venus:
    (A) Oceans
    (B) Lava
    (C) Volcanoes
    (D) Grass
    (E) Evidence of human life

3. According to the passage, who first identified that the morning star and the evening star were in fact the same celestial body?
    (A) Pythagoras
    (B) Modern scientists
    (C) Venera 3
    (D) Venera 4
    (E) None of the above

4. The author's main purpose for writing this passage is to:
    (A) Explain the mystery of why Venus has volcanoes but no lava
    (B) Give a detailed history of planetary research
    (C) To explain the origin of Venus' name
    (D) To provide general information about Venus
    (E) To compare Venus to Earth

5. According to the passage, all of the following are true about Venus EXCEPT:
   (A) The first unmanned vehicle to make it to Venus was Venera 3
   (B) Venus is actually a star
   (C) Venus is the second planet from the sun
   (D) Venus is Earth's "sister planet"
   (E) The "morning star" and the "evening star" are actually both Venus

Math Section

Math Practice Section

TIME YOURSELF- THESE PROBLEMS SHOULD TAKE YOU ABOUT 6 MINUTES TOTAL

1. If $T + 25 = 28$, then $T \times 25 =$
   (A) 3/25
   (B) 1
   (C) 3
   (D) 75
   (E) 76

2. A piece of string 3 feet long can be cut into how many 4 inch pieces?
   (A) 6
   (B) 8
   (C) 9
   (D) 12
   (E) 15

2. 712970

   ⋔ ⋔

   A B

   The value of the "7" in the A place above is how many times the value of the "7" in the B place above?
   (A) 10,000
   (B) 1,000
   (C) 100
   (D) 10
   (E) 1

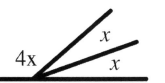

4.

Figure 1

In Figure 1 above, if 3 lines meet as shown, what is the value of x?
(A)   15
(B)   20
(C)   30
(D)   40
(E)   90

5.   If $a + b$ is divisible by 5, which of the following is also divisible by 5?
(A) $a \times b$
(B) $5 + (a \times b)$
(C) $5a + 2b$
(D) $(a+b)/5$
(E) $(3 \times a) + (3 \times b)$

Answers to Workout #4

Synonyms

1. D- benediction has the bene root that means good and also the dict root that means to speak. Literally, benediction would mean to speak good, but it has come to mean blessing.

2. B- re means again so recurrent is something that happens again and again. Chronic (the chron root means time) has the same meaning

3. A- de means opposite or away from, so devalue would be to take away value. To debase means the same thing. Did you notice that these words have the same root?

4. E- the loq root means to talk, so loquacious is talkative

5. C- a diplomat tries not to offend anyone, so diplomatic means tactful. This was one of the words to remember so make a flashcard if you haven't already

Analogies

1. A, relationship #5- a panacea is used to cure and a vacuum is used to clean.

2. C, relationship #9- the magn and mini roots have opposite meanings, so we know magnificent and miniscule must be antonyms. Abstract means not clearly defined, which is the opposite of concrete.

3. B, relationship #3- infidelity is a type of betrayal. A clown is a type of performer.

4. E, relationship #6- this is a degree relationship. To excise is to cut something out, but eradicate is to get rid of it forever. To deter is to discourage someone from doing something, but to forbid is to absolutely not let him do it. You may have chosen choice A because chronicle and record are synonyms,

however, one is not a more extreme form of the other, so choice A does not work.

5. B, relationship #12- In the question words, just one letter is changed, and choice B is the only answer choice where just one letter is changed. Choice C is tempting because the j is changed to a t, but another letter is added, so choice C does not work.

Reading Passage

1. E- the first sentence of the second paragraph restates choice E. Choice C is tempting because right after the passage discusses "sister planet", it mentions that Venus has oceans. However, it doesn't say that it was called Earth's sister planet *because* of those oceans, so choice C is wrong.

2. C- the passage does talk about the volcanoes on Venus. Don't be fooled by choices A and B. Oceans are not *currently* found on Venus, so choice A is wrong. The passage also mentions lava, but only to say that there is no lava on Venus, so choice B is also wrong.

3. A- The second to last sentence in the fourth paragraph tell us that it was Pythagoras. Choices B, C, and D are mentioned in the passage, but not as having identified the morning star and the evening star as Venus.

4. D- If we use ruling out, choice A is out because the passage tells us that there is no explanation for why Venus has volcanoes but no lava. Choice B can be eliminated because it is far broader than the scope of the passage. Choice C is out because the passage doesn't tell us where Venus' name came from. Choice E is out because comparing Venus to Earth was the topic of one paragraph, but not the entire passage. We are left with choice D, which goes well with the very last sentence of the passage.

5. B- For this one, the passage tells us that people thought Venus was a star, but it really wasn't. That means choice B is correct.

Math

1. D- first we solve for T. If $T+25=28$, then T would have to equal 3. If $T=3$, then $T \times 25 = 3 \times 25 = 75$

2. C- this is another one of those tricky problems that mixes units of measurement. First we have to convert 3 feet into inches, so we multiply 3×12 to get 36 inches.

Now we can divide 36 by 4, which basically tells us how many groups of 4 inches would fit in 36 inches. $36 \div 4 = 9$, so C is our answer.

3. A- the 7 in the A place is equal to 700,000. The 7 in the B place is equal to 70. To get from 70 to 700,000, we need 4 more zeroes, so we would multiply by 10,000.

4. C- All of the angles on one side of a line add to 180°. That means that $x + x + 4x = 180$. If we combine like terms, we get $6x = 180$. In order to get x by itself, we have to divide both sides by 6. $180 \div 6 = 30$, so choice C is correct.

5. E- For this problem, we have variables in the answer choices, so we can plug in our own numbers. Since $a+b$ is divisible by 5, I am going to make $a=2$ and $b=3$. Now I just plug those values into the answer choices and see which one gives me a result that is divisible by 5.
   (A) $a \times b = 2 \times 3 = 6$
   (B) $5 + (a \times b) = 5 + (2 \times 3) = 5 + 6 = 11$
   (C) $5a + 2b = 5(2) + 2(3) = 10 + 6 = 16$
   (D) $\frac{a+b}{5} = \frac{2+3}{5} = \frac{5}{5} = 1$
   (E) $(3 \times a) + (3 \times b) = (3 \times 2) + (3 \times 3) = 6 + 9 = 15$

Workout #5

Verbal Section

Vocab

Below are some roots. I will give you the definition of the root and then two examples of words that have that root. Look up the meaning of those words and write the definitions in the blanks provided. As you look up the definition of each word, think about how it relates to the root. After you write the definition of each word, write a sentence using the word or a memory trick or association for remembering the word.

Root: cred- believe
Credible
Definition:

Sentence or memory trick:

Creed (Yes, I know this is spelled slightly different from the root- it happens!)
Definition:

Sentence or memory trick:

Root: mal- bad
Malevolent
Definition:

Sentence or memory trick:

Malady
Definition:

Sentence or memory trick:

Word to Remember!!!

Rancorous- characterized by hostility
Ex: After Sheila's best friend stole her boyfriend, their relationship became quite rancorous.

Now, MAKE FLASHCARDS FOR ALL THE WORDS ABOVE- AND STUDY THEM!

Synonyms strategy review

If you know the word, think of a definition before you look at answer choices

If you have heard the word but can't define it:

1) Use context- in what sentence or phrase have you heard the word before?

2) Positive or negative- write a plus or minus sign next to the question word, rule out answer choices that are opposite or neutral

3) Look for roots and word parts- ask yourself what other words this word looks like

Synonyms practice.

Before you answer the question, I want you to write beside it which strategy you used from above.

TIME YOURSELF- THESE QUESTIONS SHOULD TAKE LESS THAN 3 MINUTES.

1. MALODOROUS: *Strategy:*
   (A) pleasantly fragrant
   (B) noisy
   (C) evil
   (D) smelly
   (E) plausible

2. INCREDIBLE: *Strategy:*
   (A) long
   (B) unbelievable
   (C) thrilled
   (D) timid
   (E) static

3. THICKEN: *Strategy:*
   (A) congeal
   (B) scull
   (C) mediate
   (D) confide
   (E) excise

4. INCISIVE: *Strategy:*
   (A) massive
   (B) simple
   (C) cutting
   (D) frugal
   (E) lively

5. DEGENERATE   *Strategy:*
   (A) clean
   (B) mark
   (C) drip
   (D) grasp
   (E) disintegrate

Analogies Strategy Review

1) If you know the question words, make a sentence from them.

2) If you don't know the question words, go to the answer choices and:

   A) Try to make a sentence with the answer choices. Rule out any that do not have a strong relationship. If you hear yourself using the words "can, maybe, could, sometimes", you are talking yourself into the wrong answer

   B) With the choices left, try to plug the question words into the sentence that you made with the answer choice words. Could it work?

3) If you are stuck on the last ten analogies, simply pick the answer choice with the weirdest word.

4) Keep in mind that there are weird ones. You will know it is a weird one because you will know the meaning of both question words and they will not be related.

Analogies Practice

Listed below are some of the common relationships used on this test:

#1 Occupation- one word is the job of the other word

#2 Part of- one word is a part of the other word

#3 Type of- one word is a type of the other word, which is a broader category

#4 Means without- one word means without the other word

#5 Used for- one word is used to do the other word

#6 Degree- the words have roughly the same meaning, only one is more extreme

#7 Characteristic of – one word is a characteristic of the other

#8 Synonyms- the words have the same meaning

9 Antonyms- the words are opposite in meaning

#10 Sequence- there is a distinct order that the words go in (months, time)

#11 Found in- one word is found in the other

#12 Weird ones – words that you know… and you know they aren't related

Below are sample analogy questions.

Next to each question:

A)   If you know the question words, write in the relationship number from above

B)   If you don't know the question words, write in WB (for working backwards)

TIME YOURSELF- THESE QUESTIONS SHOULD TAKE LESS THAN 3 MINUTES.

1. Pantheon is to gods as   *Relationship #/Strategy:*
    (A)   dictionary is to words
    (B)   screwdriver is to screw
    (C)   doctor is to nurse
    (D)   winter is to summer
    (E)   priest is to church

2. Health is to malady as silence is to   *Relationship #/ Strategy:*
   (A)   quiet
   (B)   reservation
   (C)   noise
   (D)   furor
   (E)   steam

3. Malevolent is to terrorist as   *Relationship #/ Strategy:*
   (A)   quiet is to scholar
   (B)   crass is to performer
   (C)   funny is to teacher
   (D)   peaceful is to pacifist
   (E)   lucky is to philanthropist

4. Rancorous is to acrimonious as   *Relationship #/Strategy:*
   (A)   belligerent is to harmonious
   (B)   shy is to athletic
   (C)   lively is to vivacious
   (D)   quiet is to determined
   (E)   lax is to successful

5. Credible is to unbelievable as   *Relationship #/Strategy:*
   (A)   kind is to popular
   (B)   erratic is to frumpy
   (C)   formidable is to weak
   (D)   culpable is to blind
   (E)   malevolent is to sinister

Reading Section

Reading Strategies

The first step when you approach each passage is to look at the questions first. You will want to label each question with either an S or a G. If it is a specific question, label it with an S. If it is a general question, label it with a G.

Then read the passage. Answer specific questions as you go. Answer general questions at the end.

Tricks for answering specific questions:

1) You can almost always underline the correct answer in the passage for these questions. If you can't underline your answer (often restated using synonyms), then you haven't found the right answer- keep looking!

2) The wrong answer choices often take the same words from the passage and then twist around the order so that they have a different meaning.

3) Look out for assumptions that you make that are not backed up by the passage

Tricks for general questions:

1) They often have the words mainly or primarily in them

2) Before answering these questions, reread the last sentence of the entire passage

3) The wrong answers are often mentioned in the passage, but they are details and NOT the main idea

Reading Practice

Below is a practice reading passage. It is an American history passage, one of the many types that you will see on this test.

TIME YOURSELF- THIS PASSAGE AND QUESTIONS SHOULD TAKE A TOTAL OF 5 MINUTES

Samuel Adams has been both a revered and reviled figure in American history. Those who place him on a pedestal as a true patriot point to his actions leading up to the American Revolution. According to their side of the story, Samuel Adams' speech against taxation without representation at a Boston Town Meeting in 1764 was designed to inspire other patriots to fight for the colonies' independence from Britain. They also view Samuel Adams as a key figure in coordinating the resistance of the colonies. To some

Americans, Samuel Adams is a brave statesman leading the colonies into a war for justice.

Samuel Adams' detractors paint a vastly different picture. In 1768, Samuel Adams sent a circular letter in an attempt to organize colonists against the British occupation of Boston. According to one theory, this circular letter led directly to the Boston Massacre. Samuel Adams also set up a committee of correspondence as a way to link patriots in all thirteen colonies. Some view this committee as an inflammatory group designed to encourage actions such as the Boston Tea Party, and eventually war. To these historians, Samuel Adams was a propagandist in favor of violence instead of reconciliation.

The true story of Samuel Adams shows that neither side may be right. There is evidence in his papers that he wanted reform in the colonies, not a revolution. As historian Pauline Maier notes, "There is no evidence he prompted the Boston Massacre Riot." What we do know is that he was a man of words, contributing to some of the most important documents in the history of the United States, such as the Declaration of Independence and the Articles of Confederation.

1. Which of the following is the best title for this selection?
    (A) Samuel Adams, a Boston native
    (B) The American Revolution
    (C) The Boston Tea Party
    (D) Signers of the Declaration of Independence
    (E) Samuel Adams, a misunderstood Founding Father

2. Which of the following words would the author most likely use to describe Samuel Adams?
    (A) Vile
    (B) Well-written
    (C) Untalented
    (D) Fortunate
    (E) Serious

3. In the passage, when the author writes that Samuel Adams has been both "revered and reviled", it is meant that
    (A) Samuel Adams has been both respected and resented by Americans
    (B) Samuel Adams actions were deplorable
    (C) Samuel Adams was an important writer in the colonies
    (D) It is now understood that Samuel Adams was a great patriot
    (E) Samuel Adams was disliked by other Founding Fathers

4. The author suggests which of the following was Samuel Adams' true goal in sending out a circular letter?
   (A) To directly cause the Boston Tea Party
   (B) It was a rough draft of the Declaration of Independence
   (C) To encourage reform and not to instigate violence
   (D) To divide the colonies
   (E) To speak in favor of taxation without representation

5. Based on the passage, what is the author most likely to discuss next?
   (A) Samuel Adams' contributions after the Revolutionary War
   (B) Other important Founding Fathers
   (C) Violence in the colonies
   (D) Samuel Adams' education and background
   (E) The importance of the Boston Tea Party

Math Section

Math Practice Section

TIME YOURSELF- THESE PROBLEMS SHOULD TAKE YOU ABOUT 6 MINUTES TOTAL

1. When 297 is divided by 32, the result is closest to which of the following?
   (A) 5
   (B) 10
   (C) 15
   (D) 20
   (E) 25

2. $0.03 \times 600.00 =$
   (A) 0.0018
   (B) 0.018
   (C) 0.18
   (D) 1.8
   (E) 18

3. The average test score for 4 students was an 80. The average for two other students was a 90. What was the approximate average for all six students?
   (A) 79
   (B) 83
   (C) 85
   (D) 87
   (E) 91

4. A telephone call is $0.50 for the first minute. It is $0.10 for each additional minute. For how many minutes could a person talk if she paid $1.80?
   (A) 10
   (B) 11
   (C) 12
   (D) 13
   (E) 14

5. What is 20% of 10% of 200?
   (A) 4
   (B) 30
   (C) 60
   (D) 100
   (E) 170

Answers to Workout #5

Synonyms

1. D- the root mal means bad, so malodorous literally means bad odor

2. B- you have to pay close attention to roots on this one. In as a prefix can mean not, cred means believe, and able means able. If you put that together, you get not able to be believed. People often say that something is "incredible" when a good thing happens, so thrilled would be a tempting choice. If we use roots, though, we know that unbelievable is a better answer.

3. A- congeal was a word to remember, so make a flashcard if you missed this one.

4. C- the cis root means to cut, so we know that the best answer would be choice C, cutting

5. E- the gen root means to create, but the de prefix tells us that we are looking for the opposite of creating. Disintegrate means to fall apart, so it is the correct answer. If nothing else, you could guess disintegrate because it has a negative root and degenerate has a negative root as well

Analogies

1. A, relationship #2- the gods are all part of the pantheon (pantheon is the group of all the gods) and words are all part of the dictionary

2. C, relationship #4- a malady is an illness, so health means without malady. Silence means without noise. If you said that the relationship was antonyms (#9), that would have worked as well

3. D, relationship #7- malevolent means evil, so it is a characteristic of a terrorist. Peaceful is a characteristic of a pacifist, or someone who loves peace

4. C, relationship #8- rancorous and acrimonious both describe bitter relationships, so they are synonyms. Lively and vivacious both describe someone who is full of life, so they are also synonyms

5. C, relationship #9- credible is something that is believable, so it is the opposite of unbelievable. Formidable means strong, so it is the opposite of weak

Reading Passage

1. E- this is a general question so we look to the last sentence. The last sentence is about his contribution to the new country. We can rule out B, C, and D because they don't even talk about Samuel Adams. The last sentence doesn't even mention Boston, so we can rule out A as well. Choice E comes closest with its reference to Samuel Adams as "founding father"

2. B- If we look for evidence in the passage, the only answer that we can find support for what the author thinks is the description of well-written. The author writes about other people who may have thought he was vile, but the author does not take a side in that debate

3. A- if you don't know what reviled and revered mean, then you have to look for evidence in the passage. After using those terms as an introduction, the author discusses people who liked Samuel Adams and people who did not. Choice A captures this meaning the best.

4. C- in the last paragraph, the author includes a quote from a historian that disproves that theory that Samuel Adams was trying to start a war. The author also tells us in the last paragraph that Samuel Adams wanted reform.

5. A- on the SSAT, questions about "what the author will discuss next" usually stick closely to what the passage is already talking about. The right answer is a continuation of thought, not a new but related subject. Only choices A and D continue the theme of Samuel Adams. It would make more sense to continue to discuss his adulthood rather than jump back to his childhood, so choice A is the best answer.

Math

1. B- the question said "closest to" so we can use estimating. 297 is about 300 and 32 is about 30, so we can do $300 \div 30$, which gives us 10

2. E- if we look at the answer choices, this is really a question about place value. If we multiply 3 times 600, we get 1800. However, since we moved the decimal two

places to the right to get 3, we have to move the decimal point back two places to the left. This gives us 18

3. B- this is a weighted average question. In order to answer these questions, we can NOT just average the two averages. Rather, we have to find the sum of all the scores. If we rearrange the average equation, we get $average \times number\ of\ items = sum$. Since 4 students averaged an 80, the sum of their scores would have to be 320. Two students averaged 90, so the sum of their scores would have to be 180. If we add these two groups together, we get that all six of their scores added up to 500. We divide this by 6 and get an average of 83 and some decimal. Since this is a multiple choice test and the question says "approximately", that is as far as we need to go. We have enough information to choose choice B.

4. E- the first minute would cost $0.50, so the remaining minutes would cost $1.30. At $0.10 a minute, you could get 13 minutes for $1.30. If we add in that first minute, we get a total of 14 minutes.

5. A- we actually have to start at the end with these types of questions. 10% of 200 is 20. Then we take 20% of that. 10% of 20 is 2, so 20% of 20 is 4.

Workout #6

Verbal Section

Vocab

This workout is a vocabulary review. Be sure to first study the meaning of the roots we have covered before you attempt this section.

Roots Review- Next to each root below, write the meaning

de _____

cis _____

fid _____

pan _____

loc/loq/log _____

magna _____

bene _____

chron _____

cred _____

mal _____

Synonyms strategy review

If you know the word, think of a definition before you look at answer choices

If you have heard the word but can't define it:

1) Use context- in what sentence or phrase have you heard the word before?

2) Positive or negative- write a plus or minus sign next to the question word, rule out answer choices that are opposite or neutral

3) Look for roots and word parts- ask yourself what other words this word looks like

Synonyms practice.

Before you answer the question, write beside it which strategy you used from above.

TIME YOURSELF- THESE QUESTIONS SHOULD TAKE LESS THAN 3 MINUTES.

1. FRUGAL: *Strategy:*
   (A)   pleasant
   (B)   distant
   (C)   restless
   (D)   economical
   (E)   functional

2. CONGEAL: *Strategy:*
   (A)   lose
   (B)   harden
   (C)   entrust
   (D)   torture
   (E)   carry

3. TACT: *Strategy:*
   (A)   sensitivity
   (B)   rudeness
   (C)   confusion
   (D)   turn
   (E)   rerun

4. SCULL: *Strategy:*
   (A)   brain
   (B)   toast
   (C)   boat
   (D)   life
   (E)   autumn

5.   RANCOROUS   *Strategy:*
     (A)   harmonious
     (B)   loud
     (C)   fun
     (D)   somber
     (E)   bitter

Analogies Strategy Review

1)   If you know the question words, make a sentence from them.

2)   If you don't know the question words, go to the answer choices and:

   A)   Try to make a sentence with the answer choices. Rule out any that do not have a strong relationship. If you hear yourself using the words "can, maybe, could, sometimes", you are talking yourself into the wrong answer

   B)   With the choices left, try to plug the question words into the sentence that you made with the answer choice words. Could it work?

3)   If you are stuck on the last ten analogies, simply pick the answer choice with the weirdest word.

4)   Keep in mind that there are weird ones. You will know it is a weird one because you will know the meaning of both question words and they will not be related.

Analogies Practice

Listed below are some of the common relationships used on this test:

#1 Occupation- one word is the job of the other word

#2 Part of- one word is a part of the other word

#3 Type of- one word is a type of the other word, which is a broader category

#4 Means without- one word means without the other word

#5 Used for- one word is used to do the other word

#6 Degree- the words have roughly the same meaning, only one is more extreme

#7 Characteristic of – one word is a characteristic of the other

#8 Synonyms- the words are synonyms

9 Antonyms- the words are opposite in meaning

#10 Sequence- there is a distinct order that the words go in (months, time)

#11 Found in- one word is found in the other

#12 Weird ones – words that you know... and you know they aren't related

Below are sample analogy questions.

Next to each question:

A)   If you know the question words, write in the relationship number from the previous page.

B)   If you don't know the question words, write in WB (for working backwards)

TIME YOURSELF- THESE QUESTIONS SHOULD TAKE LESS THAN 3 MINUTES.

1.   Beneficent is to evil as   *Relationship #/Strategy:*
     (A)   belt is to dress
     (B)   ascent is to descent
     (C)   swimmer is to water
     (D)   church is to temple
     (E)   circle is to square

2.   Deter is to encourage as irritate is to   *Relationship #/ Strategy:*
     (A)   soothe
     (B)   build
     (C)   annoy
     (D)   renounce
     (E)   stunning

3.   Deflate is to collapse as   *Relationship #/ Strategy:*
     (A)   exhibit is to paint
     (B)   rattle is to noise
     (C)   inflate is to explode
     (D)   judge is to explain
     (E)   run is to jog

4.   Beneficial is to favorable as   *Relationship #/Strategy:*
     (A)   irate is to calm
     (B)   jovial is to energetic
     (C)   conceited is to attractive
     (D)   detrimental is to harmful
     (E)   volatile is to rough

30 Days to Acing the Upper Level SSAT

5. Incredulous is to skeptic as   *Relationship #/Strategy:*
   (A) praise is to critic
   (B) fast is to runner
   (C) tedious is to police
   (D) admiring is to teacher
   (E) frugal is to miser

Reading Section

Reading Strategies

The first step when you approach each passage is to look at the questions first. You will want to label each question with either an S or a G. If it is a specific question, label it with an S. If it is a general question, label it with a G.

Then read the passage. Answer specific questions as you go. Answer general questions at the end.

Tricks for answering specific questions:

1) You can almost always underline the correct answer in the passage for these questions. If you can't underline your answer (often restated using synonyms), then you haven't found the right answer- keep looking!

2) The wrong answer choices often take the same words from the passage and then twist around the order so that they have a different meaning.

3) Look out for assumptions that you make that are not backed up by the passage

Tricks for general questions:

1) They often have the words mainly or primarily in them

2) Before answering these questions, reread the last sentence of the entire passage

3) The wrong answers are often mentioned in the passage, but they are details and NOT the main idea

Reading Practice

Below is a practice reading passage. It is an American history document, one of the many types of passages that you will see on this test.

TIME YOURSELF- THIS PASSAGE AND QUESTIONS SHOULD TAKE A TOTAL OF 5 MINUTES

The following part of a speech was given by Frederick Douglass in 1852 on the Fourth of July.

Fellow citizens, above your national, tumultuous joy, I hear the mournful wail of millions, whose chains, heavy and grievous yesterday, are today rendered more intolerable by the jubilant shouts that reach them. If I do forget, if I do not remember those bleeding children of sorrow this day, "may my right hand forget her cunning, and may my tongue cleave to the roof of my mouth!"

To forget them, to pass lightly over their wrongs and to chime in with the popular theme would be treason most scandalous and shocking, and would make me a reproach before God and the world.

My subject, then, fellow citizens, is "American Slavery." I shall see this day and its popular characteristics from the slave's point of view. Standing here, identified with the American bondman, making his wrongs mine, I do not hesitate to declare, with all my soul, that the character and conduct of this nation never looked blacker to me than on this Fourth of July.

1. Why does Frederick Douglass say that the "conduct of this nation never looked blacker to me than on this Fourth of July"?
    (A) He was speaking to an audience of slave hunters
    (B) Most of the people to whom he was speaking were not able to help slaves
    (C) Slavery still existed in the United States at the time of his speech
    (D) The Declaration of Independence had promised slaves freedom but they had not yet received it
    (E) He is personally a slave owner

2. What does Frederick Douglass mean when he says that the chains "are today rendered more intolerable by the jubilant shouts that reach them"?
    (A) Those who are slaves feel more oppressed when they hear other American celebrating their freedom
    (B) The slave masters make the slaves work longer hours since it is a holiday
    (C) It shows that slaves are not enjoying the freedom that they have been given
    (D) The audience members should not be bothered by the sound of the chains
    (E) The slaves are loudly celebrating in their own quarters

3. The purpose of Frederick Douglass' speech was to
   (A) rally the slaves to revolt
   (B) ruin the fun that the audience was having
   (C) suggest that people should go home and free their slaves immediately
   (D) point out the injustice of other Americans celebrating their freedom while slaves remain captive
   (E) encourage the party to end early

4. What is the "popular theme" to which Frederick Douglas was referring?
   (A) Abolishing slavery
   (B) Giving women the right to vote
   (C) Freedom and independence
   (D) Fireworks
   (E) Western expansion

Math Section

Math Practice Section

TIME YOURSELF- THESE PROBLEMS SHOULD TAKE YOU ABOUT 6 MINUTES TOTAL

1. $40 - 3\,^4/_{15} =$
   (A) $36\,^4/_{15}$
   (B) $36\,^{11}/_{15}$
   (C) $37\,^4/_{15}$
   (D) $37\,^2/_3$
   (E) $38\,^2/_3$

2. The average test score for two students was 80. The average test score for another three students was an 85. What was the total average for all five students?
   (A) 79
   (B) 81
   (C) 82.5
   (D) 83
   (E) 84

3. 6 is 8 percent of
   (A)   36
   (B)   48
   (C)   75
   (D)   92
   (E)   100

4. 0.1725 =
   (A) $\frac{1}{10} + \frac{7}{100} + \frac{2}{1,000} + \frac{5}{10,000}$
   (B) $\frac{1}{10} \times \frac{7}{100} \times \frac{2}{1,000} \times \frac{5}{10,000}$
   (C) $\frac{17}{10} + \frac{25}{100}$
   (D) $1 + \frac{1}{7} + \frac{1}{1} + \frac{1}{5}$
   (E) $\frac{1}{10} + \frac{7}{10} + \frac{2}{10} + \frac{5}{10}$

5. If $a > 5$, which of the following is greatest?
   (A) $(a+5)/a$
   (B) $a/(a+5)$
   (C) $a+5$
   (D) $a-5$
   (E) $3a+5$

Answers to Workout #6

Synonyms

1. D- frugal was one of the words to remember

2. B- congeal was also one of the words to remember

3. A- tact means not wanting to offend, and choice A comes closest to this meaning

4. C- don't be tricked by this one. Scull spelled with a c is a type of boat used to race crew

5. E- rancor is bad feelings, so rancorous describes a relationship characterized by bitter feelings.

Analogies

1. B, relationship #9- beneficent and evil are opposites (the bene root means good, which is the opposite of evil). Ascent and descent are also opposites, as we can tell from the prefixes

2. A, relationship #9- deter has a negative root and encourage is a positive word, so even without knowing the exact meaning of deter we can make a good guess that encourage and deter are opposite in meaning. Soothe is the opposite of irritate, so choice A is correct

3. C, relationship #6- to deflate is to slowly let the air out of something, but if something is really deflated, it collapses. If something is really inflated, it explodes, so choice C is correct

4. D, relationship #8- the bene root means good, so beneficial and favorable are synonyms. Detrimental and harmful are also synonyms. With this question, we have to be careful to look for true synonyms and not just words that "seem to

go together". Jovial and energetic could be related and conceited people may be attractive, but these words are not synonyms so choices B and C are not correct.

5. E, relationship #7- we can use roots to determine the first relationship. In can mean not as a prefix and cred means to believe. If someone does not believe, they are incredulous. This is a characteristic of a skeptic. A characteristic of a miser is frugality, so choice E is correct. A teacher may be admiring, but not always. A runner may be fast, but he may also be slow. Only a miser is always frugal.

Reading Passage

1. C- Remember that we have to have evidence. We have no idea to whom he was speaking, so we can rule out choices A and B. The passage also does not mention the Declaration of Independence or whether or not Douglass owned slaves, so choices D and E are out. He does talk about the not forgetting the slaves who are chained, however, so we can assume that slavery existed at the time.

2. A- Again, if the answer is very specific, then we have to have evidence. If you look at choice B, there is not evidence that the slaves are working longer hours (although we may make that assumption, the passage does not give us support for it). Choice B can be eliminated. Choice C can be ruled out because Douglass is saying that the slaves have not been given freedom. If you look at choice D, Douglass is saying the opposite. He is telling the audience that the chains should bother them. Choice E can also be eliminated because the slaves are producing a "mournful wail" and not celebrating. This leaves us with choice A, which goes along with the themes of the passage.

3. D- Choices A and C are too extreme. Choices B and E imply that one of the greatest Americans of all time was merely there to spoil the fun, which would definitely not be the right answer on the SSAT. We are left with choice D.

4. C- Douglass gave this speech on the Fourth of July, so the theme of the day would have been independence. Choice D (fireworks) is a trap. We may associate the Fourth of July and fireworks, but that is not the focus of Douglass speech

Math

1. B- we can use our range strategy on this one. $3\frac{4}{15}$ is between 3 and 4. $40-3=37$ and $40-4=36$. This tells us that the correct answer is between 36 and 37 so we know that it must be A or B. A is a trap- when you subtract a fraction, you generally do not wind up with the same fraction. If you find a common denominator and do the math, choice B is correct.

2. D- this is a weighted average problem. Our first step is to find the sum of all the scores. The first group has two students with an average of 80, so the sum of their scores would be 160. The second group had 3 students with an average of 85, so the sum of their scores would be 255. If we add these numbers together, we get that the sum of all five students scores is 415. To find the average, we divide 415 by 5 since there was a total of five students. This gives us an average of 83.

3. C- you can use estimating and plug in answer choices to see what works. 8 % is about 10%, so you can find 10% of each answer choice
    (A)   10% of 36 is 3.6
    (B)   10% of 48 is 4.8
    (C)   10% of 75 is 7.5
    (D)   10% of 92 is 9.2
    (E)   10% of 100 is 10

    Since 8% is a little less than 10%, I am looking for something that is a little bit bigger than 6. Choice C fits the bill.

4. A- this question tests place value. The first decimal to the right is the tenths place, the next one is the hundredths place, the next one is the thousandths place, and the one after that is the ten-thousandths place. Choice A correctly assigns the value of each digit in the number.

5. E- for this question, there are variables in the answer choices, so we can plug in our own number. The problem says that a is greater than 5, so we can plug in 6 to the answer choices.
    (A) $\frac{a+5}{a} = \frac{6+5}{6} = \frac{11}{6}$
    (B) $\frac{a}{a+5} = \frac{6}{6+5} = \frac{6}{11}$
    (C) $a+5 = 6+5 = 11$
    (D) $a-5 = 6-5 = 1$
    (E) $3a+5 = 3(6)+5 = 23$

Workout #7

Verbal Section

Vocab

Below are some roots. I will give you the definition of the root and then two examples of words that have that root. Look up the meaning of those words and write the definitions in the blanks provided. As you look up the definition of each word, think about how it relates to the root. After you write the definition of each word, write a sentence using the word or a memory trick or association for remembering the word.

Root: eu- well or good
Eulogy (Do you recognize that log root??)
Definition:

Sentence or memory trick:

Euphony
Definition:

Sentence or memory trick:

Root: neo/nov- new (do you remember this root from neologism?)
Neophyte
Definition:

Sentence or memory trick:

Novice
Definition:

Sentence or memory trick:

Word to Remember!!!

Obsolete- out of date and therefore not useful
Ex: The teenager whined to her parents that her cell phone was horribly obsolete and she needed a new one.

Now, MAKE FLASHCARDS FOR ALL THE WORDS ABOVE- AND STUDY THEM!

Synonyms practice

TIME YOURSELF- THESE QUESTIONS SHOULD TAKE LESS THAN 3 MINUTES.

1. INNOVATE:
   (A) flood
   (B) evict
   (C) sign
   (D) invent
   (E) praise

2. EUPHONY:
   (A) loud noise
   (B) pleasant sound
   (C) drill
   (D) call
   (E) uproar

3. BITTER:
   (A) rancorous
   (B) methodical
   (C) obsolete
   (D) profound
   (E) residual

4. EUPHORIA:
   (A) tact
   (B) load
   (C) jubilation
   (D) sound
   (E) felon

5. MALFUNCTIONING

    (A) operating
    (B) ignoring
    (C) flight
    (D) mean
    (E) defective

Checklist- check off the strategies that you used. If you didn't use any of these strategies, go back and look over your work!

_____ I used roots to figure out meanings

_____ I used context

_____ I used positive or negative

_____ I ruled out what I could and then guessed

Analogies Practice

TIME YOURSELF- THESE QUESTIONS SHOULD TAKE LESS THAN 3 MINUTES.

1. Obsolete is to novel as
    (A) friendly is to grumpy
    (B) humorous is to funny
    (C) unique is to solitary
    (D) liberated is to free
    (E) ideal is to uneasy

2. Tyrannical is to benevolent as impatient is to
    (A) crowded
    (B) understanding
    (C) boring
    (D) beneficial
    (E) expert

3. Eloquent is to orator as
    (A) praiseworthy is to criminal
    (B) frantic is to teacher
    (C) devoted is to indigent
    (D) conceited is to actress
    (E) beneficent to philanthropist

4. Epidemic is to pandemic as
   (A) mansion is to house
   (B) house is to home
   (C) protest is to riot
   (D) funnel is to cake
   (E) rain is to precipitation

5. Novice is to beginner as
   (A) sail is to boat
   (B) expert is to force
   (C) foundation is to roof
   (D) bend is to curve
   (E) saint is to villain

Checklist- check off the strategies that you used. If you didn't use any of these strategies, go back and look over your work!

_____ I identified the relationship if I knew the words

_____ If I didn't know the question words, I went to the answer choices and ruled out the ones that were not related or that couldn't have the same relationship as the question words

_____ I guessed if I could rule out even one

Reading Practice

Below is a practice reading passage. It is a poetry passage, one of the many types that you will see on this test.

TIME YOURSELF- THIS PASSAGE AND QUESTIONS SHOULD TAKE A TOTAL OF 5 MINUTES

Have you got a brook in your little heart,
Where bashful flowers blow,
And blushing birds go down to drink,
And shadows tremble so?

And nobody knows, so still it flows,
That any brook is there;
And yet your little draught of life
Is daily drunken there.

Then look out for the little brook in March,
When the rivers overflow,
And the snows come hurrying from the hills,
And the bridges often go.

And later, in August it may be,
When the meadows parching lie,
Beware, lest this little brook of life
Some burning noon go dry!

   - Emily Dickinson

1. In this poem, the little brook most probably represents
    (A)   a deep, dark secret
    (B)   a passion that is kept secret
    (C)   a strong river
    (D)   the autumn migration of birds
    (E)   death

2. Which of the following statements would the speaker of the poem most likely agree with?
    (A)   People should keep not let the love in their hearts die out.
    (B)   People should keep love a secret.
    (C)   People should keep wells so that they will not run out in a drought.
    (D)   Love is better when it is out in the open.
    (E)   Visiting nature is like falling in love.

3. "Where bashful flowers blow" suggests
   (A) receiving flowers is generally embarrassing
   (B) flowers are hard to grow next to a river
   (C) people have a part of their hearts that they are too nervous to share with others
   (D) the brook will swamp the flowers in the spring
   (E) a late snow can sometimes kill the flowers

4. Why do the rivers overflow?
   (A) It rained a lot.
   (B) The snow is melting in the mountains.
   (C) The speaker is angry.
   (D) Other rivers are overflowing.
   (E) The rivers did not overflow.

Checklist- check off the strategies that you used. If you didn't use any of these strategies, go back and look over your work

_____ I marked S and G

_____ I reread the last sentences before answering general questions (although this is less helpful on a poetry passage)

_____ I underlined the answer in the passage for specific questions

Math Practice Section

1. If Sam has 24 baseball cards and Hannah has 32 baseball cards, how many baseball cards must Hannah give to Sam in order for them to have the same number of cards?
   - (A) 8
   - (B) 6
   - (C) 5
   - (D) 4
   - (E) 2

2. Craig has a deck of cards that are numbered one through thirteen. If he randomly picks a card, what is the chance that the card will have an odd number on it?
   - (A) 6/13
   - (B) 1/2
   - (C) 7/13
   - (D) 8/13
   - (E) 2/3

3. At a restaurant, 24 people are waiting to be seated. There are eight tables available. If each table has at least one person but no table has more than five people, what is the maximum number of tables that can have 5 people?
   - (A) 6
   - (B) 5
   - (C) 4
   - (D) 3
   - (E) 2

4. The result of the following equation is closest to:
   25, 193 X 1107
   - (A) 27,500,000
   - (B) 25,000,000
   - (C) 2,750,000
   - (D) 2,500,000
   - (E) 275,000

5. If the average of 7 consecutive odd whole numbers is 13, what is the largest of these numbers?
   (A) 7
   (B) 10
   (C) 13
   (D) 16
   (E) 19

Answers to Workout #7

Synonyms

1) D- the nov root means new, so innovate means to make something new, or invent

2) B- eu means well or good and phon means sound (think of telephone), so euphony is a pleasant sound

3) A- rancorous is a synonym for bitter. Even if you didn't remember this, though, you should have been able to rule out some of the other answer choices and then guessed

4) C- eu means well or good, so we are looking for a positive word. Jubilation means extreme happiness, so that goes with euphoria.

5) E- mal means bad, so malfunctioning is bad functioning, or defective

Analogies

1) A- obsolete means out of date, but novel (see that nov root?) means new, so the words are antonyms. Friendly and grumpy are the only other antonyms in this question

2) B- tyrannical means really mean (think of Tyrannosaurus Rex), but benevolent has that bene root, which means good. This tells me that we are looking for antonyms. Understanding is the opposite of impatient, so that is our correct answer. It is not an exact match, but it is the best answer offered.

3) E- eloquent is a characteristic of an orator (someone who gives speeches). Did you recognize that loq root? Choices A and C have words that are not related, so we can rule those out. A teacher may be frantic and an actress may be conceited, but the word may tells us that choices B and D are out as well. We are left with choice

E. A philanthropist is someone who gives money to charities, so it would go with the bene root.

4) C- this is a degree relationship. An epidemic can grow into a pandemic (a disease that infects the whole Earth). You may have chosen choice A because a mansion is a really big house, but the problem is that the words are in the wrong order, so choice A is out. A protest can grow into a riot, just like an epidemic can grow into a pandemic, so choice C is correct.

5) D- Novice and beginner are synonyms (did you recognize that nov root that means new?). A bend and a curve are also synonyms, so choice D is correct

Reading Passage

1) B- The poem says the brook is "in your little heart" and that "nobody knows", so it is some sort of secret. We can narrow it down to choice A or B. Choice A is pretty extreme, though, with the words "deep, dark". There is nothing to indicate that it is a dark secret, so choice A is out and choice B is correct.

2) A- this is a poem, so the answer is likely metaphorical and not a literal stream running dry. The poem refers to "a brook in your little heart" and then warns us "beware, lest this little brook of life… go dry". Choice A is in line with these ideas.

3) C- Again, we need to look for the metaphorical and not the literal. Choice C is the only answer that does not talk about the literal, physical flowers, so it is the correct answer

4) B- the poet tells us "when the rivers overflow,/ And the snows come hurrying from the hills,/ And the bridges often go". The snow is melting in the mountains and flooding the bridges, so choice B is correct

Math Practice

1) D- this question is asking us for the value of a variable. Even though the problem does not assign the variable a letter, the number of cards is still a variable. That means we can plug in answer choices. We will start with C because it is the middle value. If Hannah gave Sam 5 baseball cards, then she would have 27 cards and Sam would have 29 cards. This tells us that she needs to give him less cards. Let's try choice D. If Hannah gave Sam 4 cards, then she would have 28 cards and Sam would have 28 cards. Choice D works.

2) C- if you list out the numbers 1 though 13, you will see that there are 7 odd numbers (1, 3, 5, 7, 9, 11, and 13). That tells us that the probability of choosing an odd number is 7 out of 13, or 7/13.

3) C- go ahead and draw out the tables. Draw 8 circles. In order to get the maximum number of tables of 5, we need to have the other tables seat the minimum number of people, or just one person. If we put 5 people at one table, and one person at the other 7 tables, then we get just 12 people. Not enough. So try 2 tables of 5 and 6 tables of 1. This gives us 16 people, still not enough. If you keep doing this, you will find that when you get 4 tables of 5 and 4 tables of 1, then it adds up to 24 people, so the maximum number of tables with 5 people is 4.

4) B- we can round off for this problems since we have "closest to". We can do 25,000 × 1,000 which is equal to 25,000,0000, or choice B

5) E- Since these are consecutive odd numbers, we can say that 13 is the middle number. That means there should be 3 numbers that are larger than 13. If we count up, we get 15, then 17, then 19. Since the problem asks for the largest number, 19, or choice E, is the correct answer

Workout #8

Verbal Section

Vocab

Below are some roots. I will give you the definition of the root and then two examples of words that have that root. Look up the meaning of those words and write the definitions in the blanks provided. As you look up the definition of each word, think about how it relates to the root. After you write the definition of each word, write a sentence using the word or a memory trick or association for remembering the word.

Root: bio- life
Antibiotics-
Definition:

Sentence or memory trick:

Biography-
Definition:

Sentence or memory trick:

Root: fract- to break
Fracture-
Definition:

Sentence or memory trick:

Infraction-
Definition:

Sentence or memory trick:

Exacerbate- to make a problem worse
Ex: I was already running late when a flat tire exacerbated my tardiness.

Now, MAKE FLASHCARDS FOR ALL THE WORDS ABOVE- AND STUDY THEM!

Synonyms practice.

TIME YOURSELF- THESE QUESTIONS SHOULD TAKE LESS THAN 3 MINUTES.

1. CREDO:
   - (A) philosophy
   - (B) evasion
   - (C) enjoyment
   - (D) convert
   - (E) predict

2. DISMAL:
   - (A) friendly
   - (B) angry
   - (C) essential
   - (D) confused
   - (E) gloomy

3. INFRACTION: *Strategy:*
   - (A) necessity
   - (B) transformation
   - (C) violation
   - (D) inscription
   - (E) approval

4. PANDEMONIUM: *trategy:*
   - (A) attack
   - (B) fatigue
   - (C) chaos
   - (D) party
   - (E) attempt

5. EXACERBATE   *Strategy:*
   (A) lose
   (B) worsen
   (C) dispense
   (D) reform
   (E) translate

Checklist- check off the strategies that you used. If you didn't use any of these strategies, go back and look over your work!

_____ I used roots to figure out meanings

_____ I used context

_____ I used positive or negative

_____ I ruled out what I could and then guessed

Analogies Practice

TIME YOURSELF- THESE QUESTIONS SHOULD TAKE LESS THAN 3 MINUTES.

1. Monologue is to speech as
   (A) knee is to leg
   (B) play is to scene
   (C) animal is to tiger
   (D) scull is to boat
   (E) rancor is to hostility

2. Malcontent is to unsatisfied as jubilant is to
   (A) frustrated
   (B) happy
   (C) solemn
   (D) knowledgeable
   (E) credible

3. Pine is to tulip as
   (A) tree is to flower
   (B) oak is to acorn
   (C) agenda is to success
   (D) hemlock is to rose
   (E) car is to road

4.   Neonate is to toddler as
    (A)   baby is to crib
    (B)   rebellion is to revolution
    (C)   adolescent is to adult
    (D)   city is to town
    (E)   pipe is to plumber

5.   Biologist is to life as
    (A)   forecaster is to astronomy
    (B)   physicist is to malady
    (C)   principal is to students
    (D)   benefactor is to library
    (E)   ecologist is to nature

Checklist- check off the strategies that you used. If you didn't use any of these strategies, go back and look over your work!

_____ I identified the relationship if I knew the words

_____ If I didn't know the question words, I went to the answer choices and ruled out the ones that were not related or that couldn't have the same relationship as the question words

_____ I guessed if I could rule out even one

Reading Practice

Below is a practice reading passage. It is a passage about native rituals, one of the many types of passages you will see on the test.

TIME YOURSELF- THIS PASSAGE AND QUESTIONS SHOULD TAKE A TOTAL OF 5 MINUTES

The sweat lodge has a long tradition in many cultures. In Mexico, it is called the Temazcal. This is the name that the ancient Aztecs gave to the sweat lodges that they used for medicinal purposes. Sweat lodges are also present in many other cultures, such as the Scandinavian sauna or the baths of ancient Rome. The Temazcal, however, are not used for ceremonial purposes or relaxation, but rather for curing medical complaints.

There is also a spiritual element of the Temazcal. The sweat lodges are oriented to coincide with the cosmic directions described in Aztec mythology. The fire is built on the eastern side of the lodge since that is where the Aztecs believe that our father, the Sun, rises. The door faces to the south.

The south is considered the "pathway of the dead", which begins with birth and ends with death. The center of the sweat lodge is considered to be the mother's womb.

1. This passage is primarily about
    (A) the history of the Aztec people
    (B) sweat lodges in various cultures
    (C) the Temazcal tradition
    (D) the oppression of the Aztec people by the Spanish invaders
    (E) the Scandinavian sauna

2. According to the passage, all are important to the Temazcal tradition EXCEPT
    (A) the location of the door
    (B) relaxation
    (C) the location of the fire within the sweat lodge
    (D) curing medical ailments
    (E) the center of the lodge acting as the mother's womb

3. The attitude of the writer toward the subject is
    (A) harsh
    (B) hesitant
    (C) carefree
    (D) interested
    (E) ambivalent

4. It is suggested by the passage that sweat lodges in other cultures are
    (A) used for relaxation and ceremonial purposes
    (B) used only for medicinal purposes
    (C) dangerous
    (D) oriented according to the cardinal directions
    (E) not a part of traditional culture

5. According to the passage, the doorway of the Temazcal
    I.   faces the "pathway of the dead"
    II. represents only death
    III. leads to a place representing the womb

    (A) I only
    (B) I and II only
    (C) III only
    (D) I and III only
    (E) I, II, and III

Checklist- check off what you did. If you didn't use any of these strategies, go back and look over your work

_____ I marked S and G

_____ I reread the last sentence before answering general questions

_____ I underlined the answer in the passage for specific questions

Math Practice Section

TIME YOURSELF- THESE PROBLEMS SHOULD TAKE YOU ABOUT 6 MINUTES TOTAL

1. Which of the following is less than $\frac{3}{4}$?
    (A) $\frac{6}{8}$
    (B) $\frac{10}{12}$
    (C) $\frac{18}{23}$
    (D) $\frac{26}{36}$
    (E) $\frac{33}{44}$

2. A weather forecaster claimed to have an 80% accuracy rate in his prediction of snowstorms. Last winter, he predicted there would be 20 snowstorms. If his accuracy rate is correct, and there were no snowstorms that he did not predict, how many snowstorms were there actually?
    (A) 10
    (B) 12
    (C) 16
    (D) 18
    (E) 20

3. A builder needs 62 wooden boards. If the boards only come in bundles of 12, how many bundles must he buy in order to ensure he has enough wood?
    (A) 5
    (B) 6
    (C) 8
    (D) 10
    (E) 12

4. A football team wants to add lights to their field. The dimensions of the outer perimeter of their field are 140 yards by 80 yards. If they want to place a light every 20 yards around this perimeter, how many lights will they need?
   (A) 22
   (B) 60
   (C) 80
   (D) 100
   (E) 110

5. If $3g + 6 > 15$, which of the following could NOT be g?
   (A) 3
   (B) 3.5
   (C) 4
   (D) 4.5
   (E) 6

Answers to Workout #8

Synonyms

1. A- credo has the root cred in it, which means to believe. A philosophy is something that you believe in

2. E- dis and mal are both negative roots. We can rule out choice A because it is positive and choice C because it is neutral. If you had to guess from there, you should still guess, but dismal does mean gloomy. Think about dismal weather as context

3. C- frac means to break and an infraction occurs when the rules are broken. It is a violation

4. C- pan means all, and pandemonium occurs when everything goes crazy, so chaos is the correct answer

5. B- if you exacerbate a problem, then you make it worse, so choice B is correct.

Analogies

1. D- a monologue is a type of speech given by one person. A scull is a type of boat rowed by one person.

2. B- malcontent and unsatisfied are synonyms, jubilant is a synonym for happy

3. A- this is a weird one. Pine and tulip "seem to go together" but are not actually related (remember that on this test, belonging to the same big category is not a relationship)

4. C- this is a sequence relationship. A neonate is a baby, who grows into a toddler. An adolescent grows into an adult

5. E- this is an occupation relationship. A biologist's job is to study life. An ecologist's job is to study nature. Don't be fooled by choice A, a forecaster studies meteorology and not astronomy.

Reading Passage

1. C- choice A is too broad, the passage is about just one aspect of Aztec culture. The passage mentions other cultures, but that is not the main idea, so choice B is out. Same is true for choice E. There is no mention of the Spanish invaders, so we can rule out choice D. We are left with C, which echoes the last sentence

2. B- choice B is correct because the passage specifically tells us that the purpose of the Temazcal is not relaxation

3. D- the passage is a no nonsense non-fiction passage. We can assume that the author is interested because he or she chose to write about the subject.

4. A- the first paragraph talks about sweat lodges in other cultures. Immediately after that, the passage reads "The Temazcal , however, are not used for ceremonial purposes or relaxation". The word however implies that the sweat lodges in the other cultures *were* used for that purpose

5. D- The passage tells us that the door faces south and the south is the "pathway of the dead", so I is correct. The passage also says that the pathway of the dead begins with birth, so II is wrong because the door does not represent death *only*. The passage says that the center of the lodge represents the womb, so the door in must lead there and III is correct.

Math

1. D- for this one, we need to compare each of the answer choices to a fraction that is equal to ¾.

Answer choice	Equal to ¾	Which is bigger
A. $\frac{6}{8}$	$\frac{6}{8}$	Equal
B. $\frac{10}{12}$	$\frac{9}{12}$	Answer choice
C. $\frac{18}{23}$	$\frac{18}{24}$	Answer choice
D. $\frac{26}{36}$	$\frac{27}{36}$	$\frac{3}{4}$
E. $\frac{33}{44}$	$\frac{33}{44}$	Equal

The only answer choice that is less than ¾ is choice D.

2. C- We can use equivalent fractions to set this up.

$$\frac{80}{100} = \frac{x}{20}$$

Now we can use cross multiplying to solve

$20 \times 80 = 100x$

$1600 = 100x$

$16 = x$

3. B- for this problem, the builder has to buy more boards than he needs because they only come in packs of 12. 5 bundles would only give him 60 boards, so choice A is out. 6 bundles would give him 72 boards, so choice B is the correct answer

4. A- draw this one out. It should look something like this:

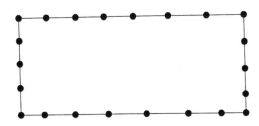

In this drawing, the lights are spaced every 20 yards and if you count up the number of lights there are 22 of them. If you try to do it the math way, it is too easy to double count.

5.   A- We can just plug in the answer choices for this one. If we plug in 3 (choice A), we get $3g+6=3(3)+6=9+6=15$. Since it is equal to 15 and not greater than 15, choice A is the correct answer.

Verbal Section

Vocab

Below are some roots. I will give you the definition of the root and then two examples of words that have that root. Look up the meaning of those words and write the definitions in the blanks provided. As you look up the definition of each word, think about how it relates to the root. After you write the definition of each word, write a sentence using the word or a memory trick or association for remembering the word.

Root: junct- join
Adjunct
Definition:

Sentence or memory trick:

Junction
Definition:

Sentence or memory trick:

Root: greg- group or to gather
Gregarious
Definition:

Sentence or memory trick:

Aggregate
Definition:

Sentence or memory trick:

Word to Remember!!!

Rendezvous- a meeting, usually in secret
Ex: Romeo and Juliet had a rendezvous that ended very, very badly.

Now, MAKE FLASHCARDS FOR ALL THE WORDS ABOVE- AND STUDY THEM!

Synonyms practice

TIME YOURSELF- THESE QUESTIONS SHOULD TAKE LESS THAN 3 MINUTES.

1. ADJUNCT:
   - (A) projectile
   - (B) associate
   - (C) image
   - (D) sum
   - (E) presentation

2. GREGARIOUS:
   - (A) complaining
   - (B) adequate
   - (C) reluctant
   - (D) social
   - (E) riotous

3. MALICE:
   - (A) hostility
   - (B) infraction
   - (C) diligence
   - (D) reward
   - (E) depletion

4. EUPHEMISTIC:
   - (A) general
   - (B) blunt
   - (C) fundamental
   - (D) truthful
   - (E) inoffensive

5. FRACTIOUS:

  (A) friendly
  (B) ill
  (C) irritable
  (D) credible
  (E) malevolent

Checklist- check off the strategies that you used. If you didn't use any of these strategies, go back and look over your work!

_____ I used roots to figure out meanings

_____ I used context

_____ I used positive or negative

_____ I ruled out what I could and then guessed

Analogies Practice

TIME YOURSELF- THESE QUESTIONS SHOULD TAKE LESS THAN 3 MINUTES.

1. Aggregate is to decentralize as
  (A) credible is to unbelievable
  (B) malevolent is to malicious
  (C) rancorous is to unhappy
  (D) gregarious is to friendly
  (E) magnanimous is to wealthy

2. Influential is to magnate as
  (A) frugal is to banker
  (B) concise is to writer
  (C) tactful is to diplomat
  (D) magnificent is to hill
  (E) eloquent is to farmer

3. Anachronism is to obsolete
  (A) restaurant is to noisy
  (B) flicker is to roaring
  (C) asset is to useless
  (D) darkness is to dawn
  (E) neophyte is to inexperienced

4. Lift is to person as
   (A) wrench is to plumber
   (B) motor is to truck
   (C) illusion is to fantasy
   (D) jack is to car
   (E) pipe is to water

5. Wave is to tsunami as
   (A) rain is to sunshine
   (B) hill is to mountain
   (C) witness is to lawyer
   (D) negligence is to care
   (E) cover is to book

Checklist- check off the strategies that you used. If you didn't use any of these strategies, go back and look over your work!

_____ I identified the relationship if I knew the words

_____ If I didn't know the question words, I went to the answer choices and ruled out the ones that were not related or that couldn't have the same relationship as the question words

_____ I guessed if I could rule out even one

Reading Practice

Below is a practice reading passage. It is an adapted folk tale from England. Folk tales are one of the types of passages that you will see on this test.

TIME YOURSELF- THIS PASSAGE AND QUESTIONS SHOULD TAKE A TOTAL OF 5 MINUTES

Carved on one of the pews in the church of Zennor in West Cornwall is a strange figure of a mermaid. Depicted with flowing hair, a mirror in one hand and a comb in the other, the Zennor folk tell a strange story about her.

Years and years ago, they say, a beautiful and richly dressed lady used to attend the church sometimes. Nobody knew where she came from, although her unusual beauty and her glorious voice caused her to be the subject of discussion throughout the parish.

So attractive was she that half the young men of the village fell in love with her, and one of them, Mathey Trewella, a handsome youth and one of the best singers in the neighbourhood, determined that he would discover who she was.

The beautiful stranger had smiled at him in church one Sunday, and after service he followed her as she walked away towards the cliffs.

Mathey Trewella never returned to Zennor, nor did the lovely stranger ever attend church again.

Years passed by, and Mathey's strange disappearance was almost forgotten when, one Sunday morning, a ship cast anchor off Pendower Cove, near Zennor. The captain of the vessel was sitting idling on the deck when he heard a beautiful voice hailing him from the sea. Looking over the side he saw the mermaid, her long yellow hair floating all around her.

She asked him to be so kind as to pull up his anchor, for it was resting upon the doorway of her house under the sea and she was anxious to get back to Mathey, her husband, and her children.

In alarm, the captain weighed anchor and stood out to sea, for sailors fear that mermaids will bring bad luck. But later he returned and told the Zennor folk of Mathey's fate, and they, to commemorate the strange event, and to warn other young men against the wiles of the merrymaids, had the mermaid figure carved in the church.

And there it is to-day for all the world to see, and to prove, to those who do not believe the old stories, the truth of poor Mathey Trewella's sad fate.

1. According to the passage, Mathey Trewella was
    (A) A merman
    (B) A farmer
    (C) A good singer
    (D) An older gentleman
    (E) A sailor

2. The people of the village had a figure of a mermaid carved into their church in order to
    (A) celebrate Mathey Trewella's life
    (B) caution other youths against the charms of mermaids
    (C) remember the beautiful female singer that had once visited their church
    (D) advise against gossiping about other women in church
    (E) commemorate the captain who was smart enough to stay away from the mermaid

3. This passage would most likely be found
   (A) in a newspaper account
   (B) in a novel
   (C) on a radio address
   (D) in a textbook
   (E) in an anthology of traditional tales

4. All of the following words can be used to describe the mermaid EXCEPT:
   (A) cunning
   (B) beautiful
   (C) wily
   (D) cautious
   (E) bold

5. A good title for this passage would be
   (A) The importance of avoiding mermaids
   (B) How mermaids trick ship captains
   (C) The grief of Mathey Trewella's family
   (D) Watch out for women who can sing
   (E) Immigration to the village of Zennor

Checklist- check off the strategies that you used. If you didn't use any of these strategies, go back and look over your work

_____ I marked S and G

_____ I reread the last sentence before answering general questions

_____ I underlined the answer in the passage for specific questions

Math Practice Section

TIME YOURSELF- THESE PROBLEMS SHOULD TAKE YOU ABOUT 6 MINUTES TOTAL

1. $1\frac{3}{5} + 4\frac{4}{5} + 3\frac{2}{5} =$

   (A) 8.8
   (B) 9.25
   (C) 9.5
   (D) 9.8
   (E) 10.125

2. All of the following are equal except

   (A) $3 \times \frac{5}{6}$
   (B) $6 \times \frac{5}{12}$
   (C) $9 \times \frac{15}{18}$
   (D) $12 \times \frac{5}{24}$
   (E) $15 \times \frac{1}{6}$

3. Ms. Smith wants to cover her lawn in sod. Her yard is 81 square yards. The sod is sold in square feet. How many square feet of sod will she need?

   (A) 27
   (B) 81
   (C) 243
   (D) 540
   (E) 729

4. Molly has a savings account that earns 6% interest in a year. If she started the account one year ago with $7500 and has not made any deposits since, how much money does she now have in her account?

   (A) $450
   (B) $7950
   (C) $8200
   (D) $8250
   (E) $8325

5. Seventeen students are on a fieldtrip to the zoo. Fourteen children want to see the lions and eleven students want to see the bears. How many students want to see the lions and the bears?

   (A) 8
   (B) 9
   (C) 11
   (D) 17
   (E) 25

Answers to Workout #9

Synonyms

1. B- the ad suffix means to or towards and the junct root means to join, so we are looking for something that roughly means joining to. An associate is someone who is connected, so that is the correct answer

2. D- the greg root means group or gather, so we are looking for a word related to getting together. If someone is social, they like to get together with other people, so choice D is correct

3. A- the mal root means bad. We are looking for a word that is very negative. Choices C and D are positive, so we can rule those out. An infraction occurs when a rule is broken and depletion is the using up of resources. While both of these are negative, they don't capture the really bad nature of the mal root. Hostility does so choice A is correct.

4. E- the eu root means well or good, so we are looking for something positive. Choices A-D are either neutral or could be good or bad. Inoffensive is a positive root in that it means not upsetting anyone. Choice E is correct.

5. C- the root frac is negative, but not overly so. We can rule out choices A and D because they are positive. Choice E, malevolent, means purely evil, which is too strong for the frac root. We are down to ill or irritable. To be fractious is to be irritable, or really grumpy

Analogies

1. A- aggregate and decentralize are antonyms. Aggregate is to combine together and decentralize is to spread out. Choices B and D are synonyms, so we can rule those out. Choices C and E have words that are unrelated, so we can also rule those out. If we use roots, it is easy to see that credible and unbelievable are antonyms, so choice A is correct

2. C- influential is a characteristic of a magnate (a magnate is a powerful business leader). The words in choice E are unrelated, so we can rule that out. If you look at choices A, B, and D, there is not a strong relationship. A banker could be frugal, a writer could be concise, and a hill could be magnificent, but the word "could" tells us that we can rule out these choices. We are left with choice C, and tactful is a characteristic of a diplomat

3. E- this one is a characteristic relationship as well, but we have to flip the words. Obsolete is a characteristic of an anachronism (something that is out of date). We just have to remember to flip the answer choices when we plug in. Choice E is correct because inexperienced is a characteristic of a neophyte (did you recognize that neo root that means new? A neophyte is a beginner). Don't be fooled by choice A. A restaurant could be noisy, but doesn't have to be

4. D- this is a used for relationship. A lift is used to lift a person (lift is another way of saying elevator). A jack is used to lift a car, so choice D is correct. The word lift has more than one meaning. Its most common meaning is a verb, but if we look at the answer choices, we can see that all of the first words are nouns. That tells us that lift must have a noun meaning in this analogy.

5. B- this is a degree relationship. A really big wave is a tsunami. A really big hill is a mountain, so choice D is correct

Reading Passage

1. C- the only answer that has evidence in the passage is that Mathey Trewella was a good singer. In the third paragraph, the passage states that Mathey Trewella was "one of the best singers in the neighborhood"

2. B- in the second to last paragraph, we are told that the carved figure was created "to warn other young men against the wiles of merrymaid". Choice B most closely restates this.

3. E- this is a folktale, so it would most likely be found in an anthology (a collection) of traditional talks (also called folktales)

4. D- there is evidence for all of the adjectives except cautious. She was very daring, so cautious is out.

5. A- choices B and C are mentioned in the passage, but are not the main idea. Choice D is too general- the passage warns us about mermaids who sing, not women in general. Choice E is way to broad- the passage is not talking about immigration to the village in general. Choice A best matches the last sentence of the passage

Math Section

1. D- let's use grouping to solve this one.

$$1 + \frac{3}{5} + 4 + \frac{4}{5} + 3 + \frac{2}{5} =$$

$$1\frac{3}{5} + 4\frac{4}{5} + 3\frac{2}{5} =$$

$$1 + 4 + 3 + \frac{3}{5} + \frac{2}{5} + \frac{4}{5} =$$

$$8 + 1 + \frac{4}{5} = 9\frac{4}{5}$$

9.8 is equal to $9\frac{4}{5}$, so choice D is correct

2. C- if we use cross canceling, we get that choices A, B, D, and E are all equal to $\frac{5}{2}$. Choice C equals $\frac{15}{2}$, so that is the correct answer

3. E- the trick to this question is that the requirements are given in square yards, but the sod comes in square feet. If the lawn is 81 square yards, then it must be 9 yards by nine yards. If we convert this into feet (by multiplying by 3), we get that the yard is 27 feet by 27 feet. To find the square footage, we have to multiply 27 by 27. Since we don't have a calculator, let's find a range. If it was 20 feet by 20 feet, that would be 400 square feet. If it was 30 feet by 30 feet, that would be 900 square feet. Since 27 is closer to 30 than to 20, we want an answer choice that is closer to 900 than 400. Choice E is correct.

4. B- we can use estimating for this problem. It is easy to find 5% and that is close to 6%. To find 10%, we move the decimal one place to the left and get 750. Half of that is 425, which would give us 5%. If we add that to her original balance, we would get $7925. Since the interest was 6% and not 5%, we want an answer that is just a little more than $7925, so choice B is correct

5. A- if we add 14 and 11 we get 25. However, there are only 17 students. This tells us that 25–17, or 8 students want to see both the lions and the bears

Workout #10

Verbal Section

Vocab

Below are some roots. I will give you the definition of the root and then two examples of words that have that root. Look up the meaning of those words and write the definitions in the blanks provided. As you look up the definition of each word, think about how it relates to the root. After you write the definition of each word, write a sentence using the word or a memory trick or association for remembering the word.

Root: doc- to teach
Doctrine
Definition:

Sentence or memory trick:

Docile
Definition:

Sentence or memory trick:

Root: mis, mit- to send
Transmit
Definition:

Sentence or memory trick:

Remit
Definition:

Sentence or memory trick:

Adept- skilled

Ex: He was quite an adept video game player. He often reached the last level quickly.

Now, MAKE FLASHCARDS FOR ALL THE WORDS ABOVE- AND STUDY THEM!

Synonyms practice

TIME YOURSELF- THESE QUESTIONS SHOULD TAKE ABOUT 3 MINUTES.

1. DISMISS:
   - (A) dehydrate
   - (B) protect
   - (C) discard
   - (D) encourage
   - (E) equate

2. JUNCTURE:
   - (A) joining
   - (B) scruples
   - (C) vacuum
   - (D) incision
   - (E) neologism

3. RENDEZVOUS:
   - (A) battle
   - (B) meeting
   - (C) forwardness
   - (D) agent
   - (E) crook

4. DOCILE:
   - (A) mundane
   - (B) strong
   - (C) public
   - (D) agreeable
   - (E) common

5. REFRACTORY
   (A) profound
   (B) gregarious
   (C) deflated
   (D) beneficial
   (E) difficult

Checklist- check off the strategies that you used. If you didn't use any of these strategies, go back and look over your work!

_____ I used roots to figure out meanings

_____ I used context

_____ I used positive or negative

_____ I ruled out what I could and then guessed

Analogies Practice

TIME YOURSELF- THESE QUESTIONS SHOULD TAKE LESS THAN 3 MINUTES.

1. Indoctrinate is to brainwash as
   (A) eulogize is to praise
   (B) expedite is to delay
   (C) run is to tire
   (D) encourage is to provoke
   (E) maintain is to abandon

2. Submit is to revoke as
   (A) accomplish is to climb
   (B) create is to schedule
   (C) excise is to cut
   (D) debase is to devalue
   (E) ascend is to descend

3. Novel is to invention
   (A) solid is to square
   (B) quaint is to city
   (C) unified is to aggregation
   (D) detrimental is to progress
   (E) found is to object

4. Missile is to rocket scientist as
   (A) car is to owner
   (B) plant is to agronomist
   (C) beach is to factory worker
   (D) teacher is to principal
   (E) chorus is to director

5. Cup is to pint as
   (A) week is to day
   (B) liter is to gallon
   (C) plate is to platter
   (D) pint is to quart
   (E) chapter is to book

Checklist- check off the strategies that you used. If you didn't use any of these strategies, go back and look over your work!

_____ I identified the relationship if I knew the words

_____ If I didn't know the question words, I went to the answer choices and ruled out the ones that were not related or that couldn't have the same relationship as the question words

_____ I guessed if I could rule out even one

Reading Practice

Below is a practice reading passage. It is a primary document written by C.J. Arthur during the First World War. Primary documents are one of the types of passages that you will see on this test.

TIME YOURSELF- THIS PASSAGE AND QUESTIONS SHOULD TAKE A TOTAL OF 5 MINUTES

I was born in November 1898 so that when war was declared I was at school. I joined the School Cadet Battalion in 1914 and was appointed corporal.

At Whitsun, 1915, I told the O.C. cadet I was going to join up. "Good," he said. "How old do you want to be?"

We fixed things between us, and armed with a letter from him, I presented myself, after attestation, to the colonel of an infantry battalion which was just being formed, and on the strength of the letter I was appointed a lance-corporal and told to get my hair cut.

I did so and afterwards saw the regimental sergeant-major, who put me through my paces and told me to get my hair cut. In ten weeks I had been made sergeant.

We did the usual training in England until May 1916, then went to France as a complete division. Some of the N.C.O.'s were sent up the line for instruction with a Scottish battalion at Ploegsteert. What a lovely war that was!

In complete daylight we marched up to and through the wood to find a network of trenches and sand-bags. Still in daylight, but now through the trenches, one was able to wander up to the front line.

During instruction with the Scottish, I was sent out on a wiring party. We were subjected to machine-gun fire, but oh, blissful ignorance, I kept upright, a perfectly good 6 feet of human target!

"Git doon, ye fool!" and, crash! my legs were knocked from under me and I fell flat on my face with a good coil of barbed wire in my stomach. The Scot explained and marvelled at my ignorance.

1. This passage is most likely to be found
    (A)   in a newspaper
    (B)   in an encyclopedia
    (C)   in a research report
    (D)   in a diary
    (E)   on a propaganda poster

2. Why does the author say "what a lovely war that was"?
    (A)   he had not yet seen combat
    (B)   the weather was nice on that day
    (C)   his battalion was winning the battle
    (D)   he was with his friends from home
    (E)   he had not yet received a promotion

3. It can be inferred from the passage that
    (A)   the author joined the army after graduating from high school
    (B)   the author was old enough to serve in the army
    (C)   the author lied about his age in order to serve in the army
    (D)   the regimental sergeant-major knew how old the author really was
    (E)   there was no age requirement for the army

4. The author's tone can best be described as
   (A) hostile
   (B) conversational
   (C) scholarly
   (D) persuasive
   (E) nervous

5. What does the author mean by "blissful ignorance"?
   (A) It is good to be uninformed
   (B) He is happy to be at war
   (C) He is happy to have been promoted to sergeant
   (D) Lacking education can sometimes be an advantage
   (E) He is glad that he did not know how much danger he was really in at the time

6. A good title for this passage would be
   (A) A history of the First World War
   (B) Soldiers go to battle
   (C) A young man's story of going to war
   (D) Changes for men in World War I
   (E) Weaponry in the First World War

Checklist- check off the strategies that you used. If you didn't use any of these strategies, go back and look over your work

_____ I marked S and G

_____ I reread the last sentence before answering general questions

_____ I underlined the answer in the passage for specific questions

Math Practice Section

TIME YOURSELF- THESE PROBLEMS SHOULD TAKE YOU ABOUT 6 MINUTES TOTAL

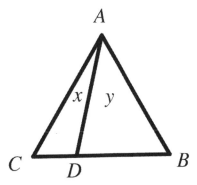

1. In the figure above, triangle ABC is an equilateral triangle, meaning that all the sides are the same length. If $2x = y$, than what is the measure of x?
    (A) 15
    (B) 20
    (C) 30
    (D) 45
    (E) 60

2. There are five students in a class. Adam is older than Bruce. Josh is older than Adam. Kara is younger than Adam. Sam is older than Kara. Who is oldest student in the class?
    (A) Josh
    (B) Adam
    (C) Sam
    (D) Bruce
    (E) It cannot be determined from information given.

3. If three numbers add to 36, which of the following must be true?
    (A) All of the numbers are positive
    (B) None of the numbers are greater than 36
    (C) The average of the numbers is 12
    (D) All of the numbers are even
    (E) All of the numbers are odd

4. In a store, some boxes have two lightbulbs and some boxes have three lightbulbs. There are the same number of each of these boxes. If there are a total of 15 light-bulbs, how many boxes have three lightbulbs in them?
   (A) 7
   (B) 6
   (C) 5
   (D) 4
   (E) 3

5. Which of the following has exactly two lines of symmetry?

(A)

(B)

(C)

(D)

(E)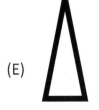

Workout #10 Answers

Synonyms

1. C- did you notice that dismiss and discard have the same root? That is a good clue that discard is the right answer

2. A- the root junct means to join, so a juncture is a joining

3. B- this was one of your words to remember, so make sure you have a flashcard for rendezvous if you missed this one

4. D- if someone is docile, they go with the flow. This is a stretch from the doc root meaning to teach, but the English language can be a quirky beast

5. E- the re root means again or back and fract means to break, so we know refractory must be something negative. That lets us rule out profound, gregarious, and beneficial (A, B, and D). if a person is refractory she just likes to be difficult

Analogies

1. A- this is a synonyms relationship. To indoctrinate a person is to brainwash, or make them believe that one way of thinking is the absolute truth. To eulogize is to praise so choice A is correct

2. E- this is an antonym relationship. To submit something is to give it to someone, but to revoke something is to take it away. Choices A and B are unrelated and choices C and D are synonyms. We can tell from the roots in choice E that ascend and descend are antonyms

3. C- novel is a characteristic of an invention (did you see the nov root that means new?). Choices A, D, and E are unrelated. A city could be quaint, but it isn't always, so choice B is out. Unified is a characteristic of an aggregation, however, so choice C is correct

4. B- this is an occupation relationship. Working with missiles is the job of a rocket scientist. Working with plants is the job of an agronomist (do you see the agr root, the same one that is in agriculture?)

5. D- there are four cups in a pint. There are also four pints in a quart, so choice D is correct. Choice B is tempting because liter and gallon are also units that measure volume, but liter is from the metric system and gallon is from the English system.

Reading

1. D- the tone of the passage is very personal and tells a story. The passage also uses the first person (or the word "I"). A diary best fits the tone of the passage so choice D is correct

2. A- the speaker talks about how he marched through the woods not yet knowing he could get shot at, so the fact that he had not yet seen combat led him to say that it was a lovely war. There is not evidence for the other answer choices

3. C- the passage tells us that the O.C. cadet asked him, "How old you do you want to be?", which implies that the author and the cadet were making up an age for him, or lying about his age

4. B- the author writes in the first person and uses included dialogue that makes it seem that he is just telling a story. This would make the tone conversational

5. E- the author uses the phrase "blissful ignorance" in the second to last paragraph. He describes walking upright even though there was machine gun fire, implying that it didn't occur to him that he could get hit. Choice E best captures this situation where the phrase "blissful ignorance" was used

6. C- choices A, B, D, and E are way too broad for this passage. Choice C goes with the very personal story that is in the passage

Math

1. B- the problem tells us that the triangle is an equilateral. That means that the sides are all equal, but it also means that all of the angles of triangle ABC are 60 degrees. That tells us that $x+y=60$. We also know that $2x=y$. If we plug in answer choice C, then x would be 30 and y would be 60. This adds up to more than 60 degrees, so we know that x must be smaller. If we plug in choice B, we get that x is 20 and therefore y would be 40. Together, these add up to 60 degrees, so we know that choice B must be correct

2. E- we can figure out that Josh is older than Adam who is older than Bruce and Kara. However, we know that Sam must be older than Kara, but have no other comparison for Sam. Sam could be older than Josh or he could be younger than Josh and still be older than Kara. Therefore, there is no way to tell who is oldest

3. C- if we look at the answer choices, for choice A, we could plug in 40, 2, and −6 and still get 36 as a sum, so we know that they don't all have to be positive and choice A is out. These numbers also allow us to rule out choice B. If we look at choice C, though, and think about what an average is, we know that choice C must be correct. To find an average, we divide the sum by the number of numbers. The problem tells us that the sum is 36 and there are 3 numbers, and since $36 \div 3 = 12$ every time, the average must be 12

4. E- we can plug in answer choices to solve this one. We will start with choice C. If we had 5 boxes of three bulbs each, that alone would give us 15 lightbulbs. Since we have a total of 15 lightbulbs, we know that choice C is too big and we should go smaller. If we plug in choice D, having 4 boxes of 3 lightbulbs would give us 12 lighbulbs. The problems said there was an equal number of boxes that had 2 light-bulbs. That would give us four boxes of 2 bulbs each, or 8 lightbulbs. If we add 12 and 8 together we get a total of 20 bulbs, which is too many. If we plug in choice E, however, we get that there are 9 bulbs from 3 boxes of 3 and 6 bulbs from 3 boxes of 2, and that adds up to a total of 15 bulbs. Choice E is correct.

5. B- choice A is a circle, which has infinite lines of symmetry, so choice A is out. Choice B has two lines of symmetry since it is an oval (go ahead and draw the two lines to prove it to yourself). Choice C has four lines of symmetry (don't forget to include the diagonals). Choice D has five lines of symmetry and choice E has only one. Only choice B works.

Workout #11

Verbal Section

Vocab

Below are some roots. I will give you the definition of the root and then two examples of words that have that root. Look up the meaning of those words and write the definitions in the blanks provided. As you look up the definition of each word, think about how it relates to the root. After you write the definition of each word, write a sentence using the word or a memory trick or association for remembering the word.

Root: ques, quer, quis- ask or seek
Inquisitive-
Definition:

Sentence or memory trick:

Query-
Definition:

Sentence or memory trick:

Root: vac- empty
Vacuum
Definition:

Sentence or memory trick:

Vacate
Definition:

Sentence or memory trick:

Meticulous- paying close attention to detail.
Ex: She was quite meticulous and never left a mess behind.

Now, MAKE FLASHCARDS FOR ALL THE WORDS ABOVE- AND STUDY THEM!

Synonyms practice

TIME YOURSELF- THESE QUESTIONS SHOULD TAKE ABOUT 3 MINUTES.

1. QUERY:
   - (A) impact
   - (B) ease
   - (C) pledge
   - (D) question
   - (E) claim

2. CONGREGATION:
   - (A) argument
   - (B) assembly
   - (C) reduction
   - (D) vacuum
   - (E) deterrent

3. EVACUATE:
   - (A) preclude
   - (B) detour
   - (C) innovate
   - (D) indoctrinate
   - (E) empty

4. METICULOUS:
   - (A) strict
   - (B) fun
   - (C) frugal
   - (D) adept
   - (E) united

5. NOVELTY:
    (A) malice
    (B) content
    (C) newness
    (D) magnate
    (E) doctrine

Analogies Practice

TIME YOURSELF- THESE QUESTIONS SHOULD TAKE LESS THAN 3 MINUTES.

1. Inquisitive is to investigator as
    (A) funny is to teacher
    (B) scholarly is to professor
    (C) scary is to holiday
    (D) confident is to actor
    (E) concise is to writer

2. Segregate is to aggregate as
    (A) combine is to join
    (B) favor is to cross
    (C) request is to submit
    (D) deplete is to increase
    (E) describe is to eulogize

3. Malign is to praise
    (A) welcome is to reject
    (B) benefit is to accomplish
    (C) excise is to encourage
    (D) malfunction is to fracture
    (E) innovate is to revolutionize

4. Journalist is to chronicle as
    (A) biologist is to lecture
    (B) plumber is to build
    (C) doctor is to treat
    (D) dentist is to encourage
    (E) editor is to write

5. Monologue is to dialogue as
   (A) speech is to paper
   (B) impression is to fact
   (C) container is to planter
   (D) malcontent is to stranger
   (E) single is to pair

Reading Practice

Below is a practice reading passage. It is a biography of an artist- one of the types of passages that you will see on this test.

TIME YOURSELF- THIS PASSAGE AND QUESTIONS SHOULD TAKE A TOTAL OF 5 MINUTES

Vincent Van Gogh was a brilliant but troubled artist who found acclaim only after his tragic death. He was born in 1853 in Groot-Zundert, Holland. From an early age, he was very emotional and lacking in self-confidence. After a series of unsuccessful occupations, he went to study art in Belgium. His goal was to bring happiness to others by creating beauty, even if happiness seemed to elude him. In Belgium, he found a community of artists that he could develop his talents with. One of these artists was Paul Gauguin. They had a close relationship, until 1888, when Van Gogh went after Gauguin with a razor blade during an argument. Gauguin was able to defend himself, but in the exchange, Van Gogh cut off part of his own ear lobe. After this, Van Gogh alternated between periods of insanity and immense creativity. He was sent to an asylum and later went to live with Dr. Gachet, who could keep an eye on him. Just a couple of months after that, he was dead by his own hand. The man whom we now consider a genius sold just one painting during his career. In 1990, however, a portrait he painted of Dr. Gachet sold for $82.5 million.

1. This author would most likely agree that Van Gogh
   (A) lived a long time
   (B) did not find fame during his lifetime
   (C) was never a good friend
   (D) was harmed by being bullied as a child
   (E) relied too heavily upon Dr. Gachet

2. When discussing Van Gogh, the author's tone can best be described as
   (A) cheery
   (B) agitated
   (C) objective
   (D) inquisitive
   (E) furious

3. Which of the following questions is answered in the passage?
   (A) How many paintings did Van Gogh sell in his lifetime?
   (B) What did other artists think of Van Gogh?
   (C) In what town did he die?
   (D) Who were his parents?
   (E) What was the subject of most of his paintings?

4. This passage deals primarily with
   (A) Van Gogh's paintings
   (B) Impressionist artists
   (C) Van Gogh's childhood
   (D) Van Gogh's various careers
   (E) The mental health of Van Gogh

5. When the author writes, "happiness seemed to elude him", it means
   (A) Van Gogh did not want to be happy
   (B) Van Gogh was happy for a time
   (C) Van Gogh didn't seem able to achieve happiness
   (D) Van Gogh lived in uncertain times
   (E) Van Gogh's family was concerned about him

Math Practice Section

TIME YOURSELF- THESE PROBLEMS SHOULD TAKE YOU ABOUT 6 MINUTES TOTAL

1. If the sides in the figure above are all 5 units long, what is the perimeter of this figure?
   (A) 20
   (B) 22
   (C) 25
   (D) 30
   (E) 32

2. A cake was cut into 24 pieces and evenly distributed among the party guests. What could NOT be the total number of guests?
   (A) 2
   (B) 3
   (C) 7
   (D) 8
   (E) 12

Questions 3 and 4 refer to the following graph

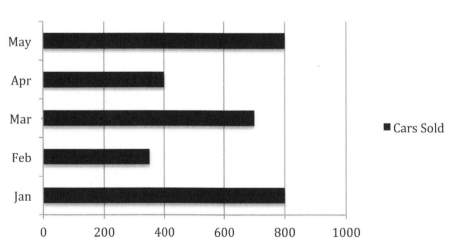

Cars Sold

3. How many more cars were sold in May than in April?
    (A) 2
    (B) 200
    (C) 300
    (D) 400
    (E) 1000

4. The number of cars sold in March is how many times the number of cards sold in February?
    (A) 2
    (B) 3
    (C) 5
    (D) 350
    (E) 700

5. A tennis player gets her serve in 80% of the time. In a particular game, her serve went in 20 times. How many times did it land out of bounds?
    (A) 5
    (B) 6
    (C) 7
    (D) 8
    (E) 10

Workout #11 Answers

Synonyms

1. D- the quer root means to ask or to seek. Choice D, question, comes closest to this meaning

2. B- greg means to gather. Choice B, assembly, comes closest in meaning to the word gather

3. E- the root vac means to empty, so to evacuate is to empty

4. A- this was one of our words to remember- please make a flashcard if you have not already

5. C- the nov root means new, so novelty is the newness of something

Analogies

1. B- inquisitive is a characteristic of an investigator by definition since an investigators job is to ask questions. Scholarly is a characteristic of a professor since it is a professor's job to be a scholar. A teacher may be funny, and actor may be confident, a writer could be concise, but these relationships are not strong enough

2. D- segregate and aggregate are antonyms. Deplete and increase are also antonyms. If you didn't know what deplete means, you could use roots to figure it out. To complete is to fill something up, but de is a negative root, so deplete is to use something up.

3. A- malign and praise are opposites. To malign something is to say something bad about it, to praise it is the opposite. To welcome someone is the opposite of rejecting them, so choice A is correct.

4. C- this is an occupation relationship. It is a journalist's job to chronicle, or record our times. It is also a doctor's job to treat. You may have been tempted by choice

E, but it is an editor's job to fix what other people have written, not to write themselves.

5. E- this is a weird one. Monologue and dialogue seem to go together, but they are both part of a bigger category (types of speeches) and that is not a real relationship on this test. Choice E is correct because a monologue is a speech given by a single person and a dialogue is a speech given by a pair of people

Reading

1. B- the passage said that Van Gogh sold only one painting in his lifetime, which is evidence that he did not find fame in his lifetime

2. C- this is a nonfiction passage, so the tone is objective. Objective means to just give the facts without taking sides, which is a good description for this nonfiction passage

3. A- choice A is clearly answered in the second to last sentence. Choice B might be tempting since we know that he did get into a fight with another artist, but choice B refers to artists in the plural, or more than one artist.

4. E- this is one of the rare passages where the last sentence does not give us the main idea. However, since most of the passage talks about Van Gogh's history with insane asylums and his random attacks, it is safe to say that the main idea is his mental health

5. C- elude means to get away. Choices D and E have nothing to do with happiness getting away. There is not evidence that Van Gogh didn't want to be happy or that he was happy for a time, so choices A and B are out. Choice C comes closest in meaning to the idea of happiness eluding, or getting away from, Van Gogh

Math

1. C- there are five sides to the figure. Each side is 5 units long. To get the perimeter we just do 5×5=25, or choice C

2. C- the problem tells us that the cake was evenly distributed. This means that the number of guests must go into 24 evenly. 7 does not go into 24 without a remainder, so that could not be the number of total guests

3. D- in May, 800 cars were sold, and in April there were 400 cards sold. The difference between these two numbers is 400, so choice D is correct

4. A- the tricky thing about this problem is that the previous problem asked just for the difference in the number of cars sold, so you have that in your head. However, they are asking for how many times, not just the difference. There were about 350 cars sold in February and 700 cars sold in March, so there were 2 times as many cars sold in March than in February

5. A- for this problem, we can set up equivalent fractions.

$$\frac{80}{100} = \frac{20}{x}$$

If we use cross-multiplying we get

$$80x = 2000$$

If we do the math, that gives us that $x = 25$. That tells us that she served a total of 25 times, and since we know that she got her serve in 20 times, she must have missed 5 times, or choice A

Workout #12

Verbal Section

Vocabulary

This workout is a vocabulary review. Be sure to first study the meaning of the roots we have covered before you attempt this section.

Roots Review- Next to each root below, write the meaning

de _____

cis _____

fid _____

pan _____

loc/loq/log _____

magna _____

bene _____

chron _____

cred _____

mal _____

eu _____

neo/nov _____

bio _____

fract _____

junct _____

greg _____

doc _____

mis/mit _____

ques/quer/quis _____

vac _____

Synonyms practice

TIME YOURSELF- THESE QUESTIONS SHOULD TAKE ABOUT 3 MINUTES.

1. RANCOROUS:
   (A) wary
   (B) confused
   (C) hostile
   (D) calm
   (E) inquisitive

2. CONGEAL:
   (A) stop
   (B) coagulate
   (C) force
   (D) vacuum
   (E) devalue

3. METICULOUS:
   (A) scrupulous
   (B) unhappy
   (C) stable
   (D) querulous
   (E) funky

4. ADEPT:
   (A) strong
   (B) brilliant
   (C) painstaking
   (D) sporadic
   (E) expert

5. EXACERBATE
   - (A) drive
   - (B) corrode
   - (C) fancy
   - (D) worsen
   - (E) strive

Analogies Practice

TIME YOURSELF- THESE QUESTIONS SHOULD TAKE LESS THAN 3 MINUTES.

1. Tactful is to offensive as
   - (A) obedient is to proper
   - (B) proud is to dismayed
   - (C) dim is to dull
   - (D) practiced is to accomplished
   - (E) concise is to serious

2. Obsolete is to phonograph as
   - (A) athletic is to marathoner
   - (B) cranky is to child
   - (C) warm is to ocean
   - (D) rancorous is to friendship
   - (E) frugal is to vacation

3. Door is to house
   - (A) window is to wall
   - (B) stairway is to basement
   - (C) hatch is to submarine
   - (D) hinge is to shutter
   - (E) roof is to mansion

4. Prologue is to epilogue as
   - (A) chapter is to book
   - (B) words are to sentence
   - (C) climax is to ending
   - (D) introduction is to conclusion
   - (E) author is to editor

5. Euphoria is to malaise as
    (A) fact is to confirmation
    (B) woe is to sadness
    (C) fortune is to wealth
    (D) intelligence is to adeptness
    (E) precision is to error

Reading Practice

Below is a practice reading passage. It is a poem- one of the types of passages that you will see on this test.

TIME YOURSELF- THIS PASSAGE AND QUESTIONS SHOULD TAKE A TOTAL OF 5 MINUTES

THE TREE

Green stood the Tree,
With its leaves tender bright.
"Shall I take them?" said Frost,
As he breathed thro' the night.
"Oh! pray let them be,
Till my blossoms you see!"
Begged the Tree, as she shivered
And shook in affright.

Sweet sang the birds
The fair blossoms among.
"Shall I take them?" said Wind,
As he swayed them and swung.
"Oh! pray let them be,
Till my berries you see!"
Begged the Tree, as its branches
All quivering hung.

Bright grew the berries
Beneath the sun's heat.
"Shall I take them?" said Lassie
So young and so sweet.
"Ah! take them, I crave!
Take all that I have!"
Begged the Tree, as it bent
Its full boughs to her feet.

1. During the course of this poem, which of the following happens?
   I. The tree dies
   II. The seasons change
   III. The birds leave the tree

   (A) I only
   (B) II only
   (C) III only
   (D) I and II
   (E) II and III

2. Why does the tree beg the wind to take the berries at the end
   (A) the tree does not want the frost to kill the berries
   (B) the birds keep eating the berries
   (C) the berries have made the tree's branches droop
   (D) the leaves have all fallen off the tree
   (E) the tree is afraid

3. In what season does this poem begin?
   (A) the dead of winter
   (B) the beginning of fall
   (C) the beginning of spring
   (D) the middle of summer
   (E) cannot be determined

4. The word "boughs" most nearly means
   (A) roots
   (B) leaves
   (C) berries
   (D) ground
   (E) branches

Math Practice Section

TIME YOURSELF- THESE PROBLEMS SHOULD TAKE YOU ABOUT 6 MINUTES TOTAL

1. If Q is the least integer greater than 3.5, what is Q?
    (A) 3
    (B) 4
    (C) 5
    (D) 6
    (E) 7

2. A lamp is on sale for $80. This is 20% off of the original price. What was the original price?
    (A) $60
    (B) $64
    (C) $70
    (D) $80
    (E) $100

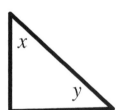

3.
    If the triangle above is a right triangle and x = y, what is the value of x?
    (A) 30
    (B) 40
    (C) 45
    (D) 60
    (E) 90

4. Of the following, which CANNOT be written in the form (3 X Q) + 4, where Q is a whole number?
    (A) 10
    (B) 16
    (C) 19
    (D) 25
    (E) 27

5. Peter is drawing a rectangle where the length and width will be whole integers. If he wants the perimeter to be 30 and he wants the length to be twice the width, which of the following could be the area of his rectangle?

(A) 10
(B) 20
(C) 30
(D) 40
(E) 50

Workout #12 Answers

Synonyms

1. C- this was a word to remember- study your flashcards if you missed this one!

2. B- did you notice how congeal and coagulate both start with co? This is not a coincidence. Congeal and coagulate both mean to thicken

3. A- meticulous means to pay close attention to detail, but you may not have known that scrupulous also means the same thing. However unhappy, stable, and funky are easy to rule out (choices B, C, and E). You may not have know choices A and D, but querulous does have that quer root which means to question. That makes it easy to rule out choice D and choose A

4. E- this was a word to remember, be sure to study your flashcards if you missed this one

5. D- this was also a word to remember

Analogies

1. B- tactful and offensive are antonyms. Proud and dismayed are also antonyms. Even if you don't know what dismayed means, you can rule out the other answer choices. Choices D and E have unrelated words (practice can lead to being accomplished, but it doesn't always). Choices A and C have synonyms. Therefore, we are left with choice B

2. A- obsolete is a characteristic of a phonograph. A marathoner must be athletic by definition. No one can run 26 miles who is not athletic!

3. C- a door is how you enter a house. A hatch is how you enter a submarine. If you didn't know what hatch meant, it could have been tempting to choose window is to wall since a window is a hole in the wall or stairway is to basement since a

stairway is how you go to the basement. However, you would have to do some real convincing to agree that these are the same relationships as door is to house. If you have to try that hard, you have just talked yourself into the wrong answer

4.   D- this is a sequence relationship. A prologue is at the beginning of a book and the epilogue is at the end. This is the same relationship as introduction and conclusion

5.   E- euphoria means extreme happiness and malaise is misery. The eu root means well or good and the mal root means bad, so we know the relationship must be antonyms. Precision and error are also antonyms

Reading

1.   B- the tree's branches bend, but there is no evidence that the whole tree dies. The birds are singing, but the poem does not mention them leaving. However, the tree has just leaves at first, and then blossoms, and then berries, so we can assume that the seasons changed

2.   C- the poem says "as it bent/ Its full boughs to her feet" is another way to say that the branches were drooping

3.   C- the tree is still green in the beginning and there are not yet blossoms. This occurs during early spring

4.   E- boughs is a synonym for branches- think of the Christmas song "deck the halls with boughs of holly"

Math

1.   B- an integer has to be a whole number, not a fraction. The smallest whole number that is bigger than 3.5 is 4

2.   E- if the lamp is on sale for $80, then the original price must have been greater than $80. Choice E is the only answer choice that works

3.   C- if it is a right triangle, then the two non-right angles must add to 90. Also, since $x = y$, we know that they must be 45 degrees each in order to add to 90

4.   E- what this question is asking you to do is figure out which answer choice could be equal to $(3 \times Q) + 4$ where Q would be a whole number. We set each answer choice equal to $(3 \times Q) + 4$ and solve for Q.

If we do choice A:

$$(3 \times Q) + 4 = 10$$
$$ -4 \quad -4$$
$$3Q = 6$$
$$Q = 2$$

Since the question is asking which answer choice would NOT give us a whole number, choice A is out. We can also see that we are looking for answer choice where we can subtract 4 and get a number that is NOT divisible by 3. 27 is the only answer choice that works (If we subtract 4 from 27 we get 23, which is not divisible by 3)

5.   E- let's make the width equal to x. This would make the length equal to $2x$.

To find the perimeter, we would do:

$$x + 2x + x + 2x = 6x$$

We know that the perimeter is equal to 30, so we set $6x$ equal to 30. That gives us 5 for x.

We therefore know that the width is 5 and the length is 10.

$Area = width \times length = 5 \times 10 = 50$. Choice E is correct

Workout #13

Verbal Section

Vocab

Below are some roots. I will give you the definition of the root and then two examples of words that have that root. Look up the meaning of those words and write the definitions in the blanks provided. As you look up the definition of each word, think about how it relates to the root. After you write the definition of each word, write a sentence using the word or a memory trick or association for remembering the word.

Root: amb/ambul- to walk or go
Amble
Definition:

Sentence or memory trick:

Circumambulate
Definition:

Sentence or memory trick:

Root: bell/belli- war
Belligerent
Definition:

Sentence or memory trick:

Bellicose
Definition:

Sentence or memory trick:

Word to Remember!!!

Wily- cunning and willing to use trickery
Ex: The Wil. E. Coyote was very wily indeed when he tricked the roadrunner into running off the cliff once again.

Now, MAKE FLASHCARDS FOR ALL THE WORDS ABOVE- AND STUDY THEM!

Synonyms practice

TIME YOURSELF- THESE QUESTIONS SHOULD TAKE ABOUT 3 MINUTES.

1. MISSIVE:
   (A) inquest
   (B) junction
   (C) animal
   (D) letter
   (E) aggregation

2. AMBULATORY:
   (A) migratory
   (B) fascinating
   (C) vacant
   (D) inquisitive
   (E) profound

3. WILY:
   (A) fast
   (B) crafty
   (C) delinquent
   (D) frugal
   (E) lazy

4. ACQUISITION:
   (A) question
   (B) doctrine
   (C) chronicle
   (D) benefit
   (E) possession

5. CREED
   (A) content
   (B) monotone
   (C) doctrine
   (D) diplomat
   (E) descent

Analogies Practice

TIME YOURSELF- THESE QUESTIONS SHOULD TAKE LESS THAN 3 MINUTES.

1. Docile is to belligerent as
   (A) harmonious is to mellifluous
   (B) harsh is to rancorous
   (C) gregarious is to antisocial
   (D) benign is to harmless
   (E) innovative is to technology

2. Tact is to emissary as
   (A) rudeness is to conductor
   (B) flavor is to licorice
   (C) plan is to battle
   (D) agility is to gymnast
   (E) mission is to spy

3. Euphony is to sound
   (A) fragrant is to smell
   (B) loud is to riot
   (C) soft is to floor
   (D) compassionate is to priest
   (E) messy is to room

4. Sport is to spot
   (A) tennis is to stain
   (B) sprint is to sprite
   (C) run is to jog
   (D) class is to mass
   (E) cord is to cod

5. Wrench is to tighten
    (A) hammer is to hang
    (B) saw is to cut
    (C) drill is to screw
    (D) wood is to tree
    (E) count is to numbers

Reading Practice

Below is a practice reading passage. It is a non-fiction passage.

TIME YOURSELF- THIS PASSAGE AND QUESTIONS SHOULD TAKE A TOTAL OF 5 MINUTES

Although he did not invent production line assembly, Henry Ford was the first industrialist to use it on a large scale. Before the popularization of the production line, most goods were handcrafted by a person who would perform every step of assembly from start to finished product. Between 1908 and 1915, Henry Ford set up factories that were radically different, however. In his factories, each person was responsible for just one step of the process. This minimized the time that workers spent switching tools or looking for parts. He also used interchangeable parts so that they could be mass produced rather than fitted for each individual car.

Henry Ford used his large factories to produce the Model T car. This new process of assembly line production allowed Ford to produce a better car in less time. These factors allowed Ford to sell the car for less, which created more buyers as more people could afford his cars. It also allowed him to pay his workers higher wages. When other companies saw the immense profits that Henry Ford realized through assembly line production, it became the standard for many different industries.

1. This passage is primarily about
    (A) The life of Henry Ford
    (B) Industrialization in the early 20th century
    (C) The development of assembly line production
    (D) The importance of the Model T
    (E) How factories work today

2. According to the passage, one of the reasons that the Model T was so successful was that
   (A) mass production produced a more attractive car
   (B) of the people who could afford cards, more of them preferred the Model T than other models not produced on an assembly line
   (C) the workers who made the Model T were paid more
   (D) it was less expensive than other cars
   (E) it had a longer lasting engine than other cars

3. This passage would most likely be found in
   (A) an encyclopedia
   (B) a current news item
   (C) a car manufacturing manual
   (D) the diary of Henry Ford
   (E) a photojournal

4. The author's attitude toward assembly line production can best be described as
   (A) disgust
   (B) awe
   (C) ambivalence
   (D) admiration
   (E) skepticism

5. What does the author mean by "interchangeable parts"?
   (A) Parts were made to fit just one car
   (B) Parts that were made to fit in any car of the same model
   (C) Parts that were handcrafted
   (D) Parts that could be used on any part of the car
   (E) Parts that were meant to last a long time

Math Practice Section

TIME YOURSELF- THESE PROBLEMS SHOULD TAKE YOU ABOUT 6 MINUTES TOTAL

1. Which of the following is closest to .24 X 41?
   (A) ¼ of 40
   (B) ¼ of 44
   (C) ½ of 40
   (D) ½ of 44
   (E) 4 divided by 40

2. If ½ of a number is less than 16, than the number CANNOT be
   (A) less than 32
   (B) equal to 32
   (C) less than 8
   (D) equal to 8
   (E) equal to zero

3. 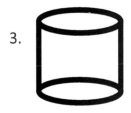 If a hollow plastic tube (shown at left) was placed on a piece of paper, which picture represents all the points where the tube touches the paper?

   (A)

   (B)

   (C)

   (D)

   (E)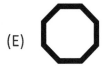

4. In a particular city, out of every 1,000 homes, 2.5 of them have a dog. If there are 2 million homes, how many of them have a dog?
   (A) 5
   (B) 50
   (C) 500
   (D) 5000
   (E) 50000

5. If x, y, and z are consecutive numbers, which of the following must be true?
   (A) xyz must be positive
   (B) xyz must be negative
   (C) $x + y + z$ cannot equal zero
   (D) $x + y$ is greater than z
   (E) none of the above

Workout #13 Answers

Synonyms

1. D- the mis/mit root means to send. You send a letter, so choice D is correct

2. A- the amb root means to walk or go, migratory describes a person or animal that moves around frequently (think of a bird migrating)

3. B- this one is a little tricky because crafty does not mean good at crafts. Crafty means scheming, or wily

4. E- to acquire something is to get it, or to take it into your possession. An acquisition is something that you have acquired, or a possession

5. C- creed comes from the cred root, which means to believe. A doctrine is also something that you believe in (a doctrine is a set of beliefs that is usually pretty strict)

Analogies

1. C- docile and belligerent are antonyms (docile means calm and belligerent means looking for a fight- do you see that bell root?). Using roots, we can see that gregarious and antisocial are also antonyms. Greg means to gather, but anti means not so antisocial means not social

2. D- tact is a characteristic of an emissary (an emissary is someone that one country sends to another country to build relations). Agility is a characteristic of a gymnast (agility is flexibility, so by definition a gymnast must be agile)

3. A- euphony is a pleasant sound (eu means well or good and phon means sound). Fragrant is a pleasant smell.

4. E- this is a weird one. In the question word, we lose an r as the second to last letter. Choice E has this same relationship

5. B- a wrench is used to tighten. A saw is used to cut. Don't be fooled by choices A and C. You might use a hammer to hang a picture, but if you were asked the primary use for a hammer, would you say "to hang"? And a drill is used to make a hole so you can screw, it is a screwdriver's job to screw and not a drill's

Reading

1. C- if we look at the last sentence, we can see that the passage was about assembly line construction. The passage does mention Henry Ford and the Model T, but those are not the main idea

2. D- the passage reads, "These factors allowed Ford to sell the car for less". This gives us evidence for choice D. There is simply no evidence in the passage for the other answer choices.

3. A- this passage gives us a summary, which is what an encyclopedia article does. It wouldn't be a current news item because assembly line production was developed a long time ago. It wouldn't be in a manual because a manual gives step by step instructions. A diary would be personal in tone and a photojournal would be just pictures. We are left with choice A

4. D- the tone is definitely positive. That leaves us with choices B and D. The word awe, however, is strongly positive and too extreme for a passage on this test. Admiration is positive but not over the top, so choice D is correct

5. B- the passages tell says that interchangeable parts "could be mass produced rather than fitted for each individual car". Choice B restates this

Math

1. A- .24 can be rounded off to ¼ and 41 can be rounded to 40. Choice A is correct

2. B- we can translate "1/2 of a number is less than 16" into an equation:

$$\frac{1}{2}x < 16$$

To get x by itself, we multiply both sides by 2. This gives us:

$x < 32$.

Since we are looking for what CANNOT work, choice B is correct. The number has to be less than 32, not equal to 32

3. A- the problem tells us that the tube was hollow, so we can rule out choices B and D. This problem is basically asking us to translate between a 3-D picture and a 2-D picture. In the 3-D picture, the bottom looks like an oval, but that is how we represent a circle in 3-D in order to show depth. A tube is actually round, so choice A is correct

4. D- we can set up equivalent fractions to solve this one:

$$\frac{2.5}{1000} = \frac{x}{2{,}000{,}000}$$

Since we are not allowed to use a calculator on this test, my first step will be to multiply both sides by 1,000 so we can get rid of some of those zeros. That leaves us with:

$$\frac{2.5}{1} = \frac{x}{2{,}000}$$

If we use cross-multiplying, we get:

$$2.5 \times 2{,}000 = x$$

If we do the math, we get that there would be 5,000 homes with dogs, or choice D

5. E- since this is a must be true problem, we need to plug in our own numbers to try to disprove each answer choice. If we plugged in -1, 0, and 1, we would get that $xyz = 0$. This allows us to rule out choice A and B since zero is neither positive nor negative. This would also make $x + y + z = 0$, so we can rule choice C. In this case, $x + y$ would also not be greater than z, so choice D is out. That leaves us with choice E

Workout #14

Verbal Section

Vocab

Below are some roots. I will give you the definition of the root and then two examples of words that have that root. Look up the meaning of those words and write the definitions in the blanks provided. As you look up the definition of each word, think about how it relates to the root. After you write the definition of each word, write a sentence using the word or a memory trick or association for remembering the word.

Root: cert- sure
Ascertain
Definition:

Sentence or memory trick:

Certify-
Definition:

Sentence or memory trick:

Root: mon- advise
Remonstrance
Definition:

Sentence or memory trick:

Admonish
Definition:

Sentence or memory trick:

Capricious- Unpredictable or impulsive

Ex: Many young celebrities are known for their capricious behavior; they have a new boyfriend and a new hair color every week.

Now, MAKE FLASHCARDS FOR ALL THE WORDS ABOVE- AND STUDY THEM!

Synonyms practice

TIME YOURSELF- THESE QUESTIONS SHOULD TAKE ABOUT 3 MINUTES.

1. WILY:
   - (A) ambulatory
   - (B) certain
   - (C) crowded
   - (D) cunning
   - (E) gregarious

2. ASCERTAIN:
   - (A) determine
   - (B) question
   - (C) accuse
   - (D) dismiss
   - (E) disprove

3. SOMNAMBULATE:
   - (A) remit
   - (B) sleepwalk
   - (C) freeze
   - (D) covet
   - (E) rebel

4. INQUEST:
   - (A) malady
   - (B) defense
   - (C) investigation
   - (D) trial
   - (E) eulogy

5. INTERMITTENT:
   (A) content
   (B) novel
   (C) benevolent
   (D) tactful
   (E) sporadic

Analogies Practice

TIME YOURSELF- THESE QUESTIONS SHOULD TAKE LESS THAN 3 MINUTES.

1. Preamble is to conclusion
   (A) prologue is to epilogue
   (B) chapter is to book
   (C) author is to writing
   (D) book is to store
   (E) fiction is to nonfiction

2. Certain is to unsure
   (A) confident is to athletic
   (B) solid is to plain
   (C) magnanimous is to benevolent
   (D) difficult is to docile
   (C) gregarious is to funny

3. Vacant is to occupants
   (A) frustrated is to anger
   (B) quiet is to noise
   (C) frank is to politics
   (D) fortunate is to wealth
   (E) fantastic is to clean

4. Question is to exam
   (A) quiz is to test
   (B) front is to back
   (C) inquiry is to attack
   (D) sock is to foot
   (E) note is to song

5. Mislead is to defraud
   - (A) lie is to certify
   - (B) last is to crumble
   - (C) object is to rebel
   - (D) fume is to consider
   - (E) collide is to fracture

Reading Practice

Below is a practice reading passage. It is from an essay by Arthur Christopher Benson.

TIME YOURSELF- THIS PASSAGE AND QUESTIONS SHOULD TAKE A TOTAL OF 5 MINUTES

There are many motives that impel us to travel, to change our sky, as Horace calls it—good motives and bad, selfish and unselfish, noble and ignoble. With some people it is pure restlessness; the tedium of ordinary life weighs on them, and travel, they think, will distract them; people travel for the sake of health, or for business reasons, or to accompany some one else, or because other people travel. And these motives are neither good nor bad, they are simply sufficient. Some people travel to enlarge their minds, or to write a book; and the worst of travelling for such reasons is that it so often implants in the traveler, when he returns, a desperate desire to enlarge other people's minds too. Unhappily, it needs an extraordinary gift of vivid description and a tactful art of selection to make the reflections of one's travels interesting to other people.

1. The author implies that most writing about travelling
   - (A) is well written
   - (B) bores the reader
   - (C) sells well in bookstores
   - (E) lacks enough detail
   - (E) is well received by the press

2. This passage is primarily about
   - (A) Horace
   - (B) specific travels that the author has taken
   - (C) the history of travel writing
   - (D) the reasons that people travel and write about it
   - (E) what makes good travel writing

3. In the passage, all of the following reasons are given for travelling EXCEPT
   (A) the dullness of routine life
   (B) well-being
   (C) migration
   (D) monetary gains
   (E) education

4. The author's tone can best be described as
   (A) humorous
   (B) malicious
   (C) ambivalent
   (D) bitter
   (E) rowdy

Math Practice Section

TIME YOURSELF- THESE PROBLEMS SHOULD TAKE YOU ABOUT 6 MINUTES TOTAL

1. Which of the following are greater than $\frac{1}{2}$?
   (A) $\frac{9}{20}$
   (B) $\frac{16}{33}$
   (C) $\frac{101}{202}$
   (D) $\frac{8}{15}$
   (E) $\frac{12}{25}$

2. There are 14 students in Ms. Smith's class. They sold an average of 4 rolls of wrapping paper for the school fundraiser. How many total did they sell?
   (A) 4
   (B) 14
   (C) 28
   (D) 36
   (E) 56

3. The population of a town increased from 3,500 in 1990 to 7 million in 2010. How many times greater was the population in 2010 than in 1990?
   (A) 100
   (B) 200
   (C) 500
   (D) 2,000
   (E) 20,000

4. If $q = 3r + 7$, what does $q - 2$ equal?
    (A) $3r + 9$
    (B) $3r + 5$
    (C) $6r + 7$
    (D) $6r + 5$
    (E) It cannot be determined by information given

5. In a particular school, 1/3 of the students walk, 1/6 of them are driven by their parents, and the remainder ride the bus. If four students are driven by their parents, how many students ride the bus?
    (A) 4
    (B) 6
    (C) 8
    (D) 12
    (E) 16

Workout #14 Answers

Synonyms

1. D- this was a word to remember, so study your flashcards if you missed this one

2. A- the cert root means sure, so to ascertain is to make sure, or to determine

3. B- amb means to walk or go, and sleepwalk is the only answer choice that captures this meaning (somn means to sleep)

4. C- the ques root means to ask or to seek. An inquest seeks answers and so does an investigation

5. E- intermittent means off and on (or not steady) and so does sporadic

Analogies

1. A- a preamble comes before a piece of writing and the conclusion comes at the end, so this is a sequence relationship. A prologue comes at the beginning of the book and the epilogue comes at the end so choice A is correct

2. D- certain and unsure are antonyms. Choices A, B, and E have words that are unrelated. Choice C has synonyms. Only choice D has antonyms

3. B- vacant means without occupants. Quiet means without noise

4. E- questions make up an exam and notes make up a song

5. C- this is a degree relationship. To mislead is to let someone believe something that is not true, but to defraud is to mislead someone with malicious intentions. To object is to think that another person is wrong, to rebel is to think that they are so wrong that you act out against them. The trick to this one is knowing that object has more than one meaning. It can be a noun or a verb

Reading

1. B- if we look at the last sentence of the passage, the author says that is very hard to make travel writing "interesting to other people". This idea is restated in choice B

2. D- the first half of the passage talks about why people travel and the second half talks about why people write about it. Choice D restates this

3. C- there is evidence of all the answer choices except choice C

4. A- the author seems to be sharing a joke with us, so the tone is humorous. Students usually have trouble identifying when adults are trying to be funny, though, so ruling out may be the best strategy on this question. Malicious, bitter, and rowdy are all too extreme for the SSAT. Ambivalence means that an author can't decide whether something is good or bad, which is not the case in this passage. We are left with humorous

Math

1. D- to answer this question, we can write fractions that are equivalent to ½ next to each answer choice and then compare

Answer choice	Equal to ½	Which is greater?
A. $\frac{9}{20}$	$\frac{10}{20}$	$\frac{10}{20}$
B. $\frac{16}{33}$	$\frac{16}{32}$	$\frac{16}{32}$
C. $\frac{101}{202}$	$\frac{101}{202}$	Equal
D. $\frac{8}{15}$	$\frac{8}{16}$	Answer choice!
E. $\frac{12}{25}$	$\frac{12}{24}$	$\frac{12}{24}$

2. E- if we rearrange the equation $average = sum \div number\ of\ numbers$, we get $average \times number\ of\ numbers = sum$. If we plug the numbers from our problem into this equation, we get $4 \times 14 = sum = 56$ rolls of wrapping paper

3. D- we can set up the equation:

    $3,500x = 7,000,000$

    To make our life easier, the first thing to do is divide both sides by 100 to get rid of some of those zeroes. We are left with:

    $35x = 70,000$

    Now we can divide both sides by 35 and we get 2,000 so the correct answer is choice D

4. B- in order to get $q-2$, we have to subtract 2 from each side. This gives us:

    $q - 2 = 3r + 7 - 2$ or

    $q - 2 = 3r + 5$, which is choice B

5. D- to solve this problem, we need to give all of the fractions a common denominator, which in this case would be 6. Since $\frac{1}{3} = \frac{2}{6}$, we know that $\frac{2}{6}$ of the students walk, $\frac{1}{6}$ of the students are driven, which leaves $\frac{3}{6}$ of the students to ride the bus. If $\frac{1}{6} = 4$ students who are driven, then $\frac{2}{6} = 8$ students who walk, and $\frac{3}{6} = 12$ students who ride the bus so choice D is correct

Workout #15

Verbal Section

Vocab

Below are some roots. I will give you the definition of the root and then two examples of words that have that root. Look up the meaning of those words and write the definitions in the blanks provided. As you look up the definition of each word, think about how it relates to the root. After you write the definition of each word, write a sentence using the word or a memory trick or association for remembering the word.

Root: pel- drive
Propel
Definition:

Sentence or memory trick:

Expel
Definition:

Sentence or memory trick:

Root: tort/tors- twist
Contort
Definition:

Sentence or memory trick:

Tortuous
Definition:

Sentence or memory trick:

Word to Remember!!!

Sporadic- Not happening regularly
Ex: He was not the most committed player on the team; his attendance at practice was sporadic.

Now, MAKE FLASHCARDS FOR ALL THE WORDS ABOVE- AND STUDY THEM!

Synonyms practice

TIME YOURSELF- THESE QUESTIONS SHOULD TAKE ABOUT 3 MINUTES.

1. CAPRICIOUS:
   - (A) impulsive
   - (B) fair
   - (C) stunning
   - (D) weary
   - (E) grumpy

2. RENDEZVOUS:
   - (A) lousy timing
   - (B) long drive
   - (C) morbid fascination
   - (D) secret meeting
   - (E) slow healing

3. PREMONITION:
   - (A) depth
   - (B) forewarning
   - (C) stalemate
   - (D) scruples
   - (E) negotiation

4. DEMISE:
   - (A) dispatch
   - (B) vitality
   - (C) assistance
   - (D) progress
   - (E) termination

5. VACUOUS:
    (A) constructive
    (B) petty
    (C) empty
    (D) concise
    (E) proud

Analogies Practice

TIME YOURSELF- THESE QUESTIONS SHOULD TAKE LESS THAN 3 MINUTES.

1. Propel is to stop
    (A) expel is to limit
    (B) fund is to spend
    (C) aggregate is to segregate
    (D) monitor is to watch
    (E) malign is to deter

2. Contort is to bend
    (A) deplete is to use up
    (B) stifle is to encourage
    (C) finish is to begin
    (D) grate is to enjoy
    (E) grasp is to destroy

3. Satellite is to orbit
    (A) earth is to moon
    (B) rocket is to propulsion
    (C) comedian is to laugh
    (D) star is to milky way
    (E) racecar is to track

4. Peaceful is to sanctuary
    (A) calm is to ocean
    (B) ornate is to ballroom
    (C) clean is to gym
    (D) sloppy is to student
    (E) furnished is to studio

5. Soothe is to exacerbate
    (A) force is to contain
    (B) smile is to grin
    (C) amble is to walk
    (D) rebel is to obey
    (E) certify is to inquire

Reading Practice

Below is a practice reading passage. It is from *Marco Paul's Adventures in Pursuit of Knowledge*.

TIME YOURSELF- THIS PASSAGE SHOULD TAKE YOU ABOUT SIX MINUTES

One summer, Forester and Marco Paul formed a plan for going to Quebec. Marco was very much interested in going to Quebec, as he wanted to see the fortifications. Forester had told him that Quebec was a strongly-fortified city, being a military post of great importance, belonging to the British government. Marco was very much pleased at the idea of seeing the fortifications, and the soldiers that he supposed must be placed there to defend them.

On their way to Quebec, they had to sail up the Kennebec in a steamboat. As they were passing along, Marco and Forester sat upon the deck. It was a pleasant summer morning. They had been sailing all night upon the sea, on the route from Boston to the mouth of the Kennebec. They entered the mouth of the Kennebec very early in the morning, just before Forester and Marco got up. And thus it happened that when they came up upon the deck, they found that they were sailing in a river. The water was smooth and glassy, shining brilliantly under the rays of the morning sun, which was just beginning to rise.

The shores of the river were rocky and barren. Here and there, in the coves and eddies, were what appeared to Marco to be little fences in the water. Forester told him that they were for catching fish. The steamboat moved very slowly, and every moment the little bell would ring, and the engine would stop. Then the boat would move more slowly still, until the bell sounded again for the engine to be put in motion, and then the boat would go on a little faster.

"What makes them keep stopping?" said Marco.

"The water is very low this morning," said Forester, "and they have to proceed very carefully, or else they will get aground."

"What makes the water so low now?" asked Marco.

"There are two reasons," replied Forester. "It is late in the summer, and the streams and springs are all low; so that there is but little water to come down from the country above. Then, besides, the tide is low this morning in the sea, and that causes what water there is in the bed of the river to run off into the sea."

"Is not there any tide in the river?" asked Marco.

"No," said Forester, "I suppose there is not, strictly speaking. That is, the moon, which attracts the waters of the ocean, and makes them rise and fall in succession, produces no sensible effect upon the waters of a river. But then the rise and fall of the sea itself causes all rivers to rise and fall near their mouths, and as far up as the influence of the sea extends. You see, in fact, that it must be so."

1. It can be inferred from the passage that Marco
    (A)   has run away from home
    (B)   is interested in the military
    (C)   is a sailor
    (D)   frequently travels to Quebec
    (E)   is a scientist by profession

2. According to the passage, tides affect rivers
    (A)   not at all
    (B)   only in the spring and summer
    (C)   along the whole length of the river
    (D)   only near where the river meets the sea
    (E)   only in the Northern hemisphere

3. According to the passage, a bell rings in order to
    (A)   warn the steamboat captain that the water was too shallow to keep the engine running
    (B)   wake the passengers
    (C)   let the fishermen know when a fish had been caught in the fences
    (D)   let the soldiers in Quebec know that a boat was approaching
    (E)   warn the captain that there was a high tide

4. Marco and Forester's journey can best be described as
   (A) harrowing
   (B) dangerous
   (C) long
   (D) pleasant
   (E) boring

5. A good title for this piece would be:
   (A) "Ninety days to Quebec: a rough journey"
   (B) "A journey up the Kennebec"
   (C) "Early fortifications in Quebec"
   (D) "Two boys on the loose"
   (E) "A history of the Kennebec River"

Math Practice Section

TIME YOURSELF- THESE PROBLEMS SHOULD TAKE YOU ABOUT 6 MINUTES TOTAL

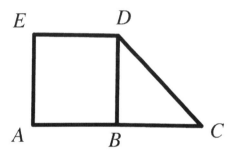

1. If ABDE is a square and AB is equal in length to BC, which of the following paths is the longest?
   (A) A to B to D to E
   (B) A to E to D to B
   (C) B to D to E to A
   (D) A to E to D to C
   (E) C to B to A to E

2. Which of the following is 3.03 closest to?
   (A) 3
   (B) 3.3
   (C) 3.4
   (D) 4
   (E) 30

3. If $3 + (A + B) = 10$, and B is greater than zero, which of the following could A NOT be?
   (A) 7
   (B) 6
   (C) 3.3
   (D) 2
   (E) 0

4.
   In the figure above, the distance from A to C is 30 and the distance from A to B is half the distance from B to C. If the distance from A to D is 40, what is the distance from B to D?
   (A) 40
   (B) 30
   (C) 20
   (D) 15
   (E) 10

5. Amy sent out invitations for her birthday party. On the invitations, she wrote that each person could bring up to two siblings. What is the maximum number of guests that Amy could expect if x is the number of invitations sent?
   (A) x
   (B) $x + 2$
   (C) $2x + 2$
   (D) $2x + 4$
   (E) $3x$

Workout #15 Answers

Synonyms

1. A- this was a word to remember, study your flashcards if you missed this one

2. D- another word to remember

3. B- pre means before and mon means to advise. Premonition therefore means an advisement before something happens, or a forewarning (fore also means before)

4. E- the root de means down or away and mis means to send. Demise is the end of something, or the termination (term also means to end)

5. C- the vac root means empty, so vacuous means empty

Analogies

1. C- propel has the roots pro and pel. Pro is a positive root and pel means to drive, so propel means to drive forward, which is the opposite of stop. Aggregate is also the opposite of segregate

2. A- contort and bend are synonyms (did you recognize that tort root that means to twist?). Deplete and use up also mean the same thing

3. E- a satellite is used for orbit and a rocket is used for propulsion. Earth and moon may have been tempting because they seem to go with satellite and orbit. However, the earth is not used for moon

4. B- peaceful is a characteristic of a sanctuary. Ornate is a characteristic of a ball-room- ballrooms are not built that are not ornate

5. D- soothe and exacerbate are antonyms. Rebel and obey are also antonyms (did you see that bell root?)

Reading

1. B- the second sentence of the passage tells us that Marco wanted to go to Quebec to see the fortifications, so we can assume that he is interested in the military. There is not evidence for the other answer choices

2. D- the passage tells us that "rivers rise and fall near their mouths", which is another way of saying where the river meets the sea

3. A- the passage tells us that when the bell rings the boat stops and that the boat stops when there is danger of running aground. We can put the pieces together that the bell is warning the captain that the water is shallow

4. C- the passage tells us that the boat moves very slowly and keeps stopping, so we can assume that the journey is long

5. B- this passage describes going up the Kennebec river, so choice B is the best answer

Math

1. D- this question is testing whether or not you recognize that the hypotenuse of a right triangle is longer than either side. All of the answer choices require you to trace three segments, but because segment DC is the hypotenuse, and only choice D has segment DC in it, then choice D is the longest

2. A- 3.03 is between 3.0 and 3.1, so answer choice A is correct. Don't be fooled by choice B, the value is very different if you take out that middle 0.

3. A- First, we have to get $A + B$ by itself. If we subtract 3 from both sides, we get that $A + B = 7$. The problem tells us that B must be greater than zero, but if A was equal to 7, then B would be zero. Therefore, A can NOT be 7, so choice A is correct

4. B- if A to C is 30, and AB is half as long as BC, then AB would have to be 10 and BC would have to be 20. If AC is 30 and AD is 40, then CD would be 10. To get the distance from B to D, we add BC (20) and CD (10) and get 30, or answer choice B

5. E- Let's plug in our own numbers since there are variables in the answer choices. If Amy invites three friends, then they could bring 6 siblings, and she would have a total of 9 guests. Let's plug in 3 for x and see what gives us 9. Only choice E does. By the way, if you had plugged in 2 for x, you would have gotten that both choices D and E would work. If this happens, you simply plug in another number until you can rule out down to one answer choice

Appendix A

Tips For the Writing Sample

Please Note: The writing sample on the Upper Level SSAT was updated for the 2012-2013 testing season. The advice and information in this book is up to date, but books from other publishers may not have been updated yet, so do not be alarmed if the information in this book and others does not match. You can always check *www.SSAT.org* if you have any questions since that is the official website of the SSATB.

When you take the SSAT, you will be asked to complete a writing sample. You will be given 25 minutes and two pages to write your response.

With the recently redesigned writing sample, you will be given a choice between an essay topic and a creative topic.

The questions are relatively open ended. The old topics were simply statements that you had to agree or disagree with- quite snooze worthy. The new prompts give you much more room to show your creativity, even if you choose the essay prompt.

So what kind of questions can you expect to see?

For the essay prompt, you might see questions like:

- What would you change about your school and why?

- If you could relive one day, what day would it be and why would you want to do it over?

For the creative prompts, they might look like "story starters" that a teacher may have used in your school. The test writers will give you a starting sentence and you take it from there.

Here are some examples of what these questions could look like:

- A strange wind blew through town on that Thursday night.

- He thought long and hard before slowly opening the door.

- She had never been in an experience quite like this before.

To approach the writing sample, follow this four step plan:

Step 1: Choose Topic

- There is no "right" choice when deciding between an essay or fiction prompt.

- If you are extremely creative and love playing with language, the fiction prompt is a great way to showcase this talent. This talent may not appear elsewhere on your application, so here is your chance.

- If you are great at organizing ideas and developing examples, the essay prompt may be for you.

- If you do decide ahead of time whether to write about the creative or essay prompt, be flexible. You may get to the test, read the creative prompt and just take off with it. Alternatively, you may read the creative prompt and have nothing, but the essay prompt looks intriguing.

Step 2: Plan

- Take just a couple of minutes and plan, it will be time well spent.

- If you are writing an essay, plan out what your main point (thesis) will be and what examples you are going to use

- If you are writing from the creative prompt, decide where your story is going. You want to build to a climax, so decide ahead of time what that will be. You don't want lots of descriptive language that goes nowhere. Decide what your problem will be and how you intend to resolve it.

Step 3: Write

- Break your writing into paragraphs- don't do a two page blob.

- If you are writing an essay topic, aim for 4-5 paragraphs (introduction, 2-3 body paragraphs, and a conclusion)

- If you choose a creative topic, remember to start new paragraphs for dialogue and to break up long descriptions.

- Write legibly. It does not have to be perfect and schools know that you are writing with a time limit. But if the admissions officers can't read what you wrote, they can't judge it.

Step 4: Edit/Proofread

- Save a couple of minutes for the end to look over your work.

- You won't be able to do a major editing job where you move around sentences and rewrite portions.

- Look for where you may have left out a word or misspelled something. If a word is not legible, fix that.

- Make your marks simple and clear. If you need to take something out, just put a single line through it. Use a carat to insert words that you forgot.

The writing sample is not graded, but the schools that you apply to do receive a copy.

So what are schools looking for?

1. **Organization**

   Schools want to see that you can organize your thoughts before writing.

   If you choose the essay topic, shoot for a 4-5 paragraph essay. There should be an introductory paragraph with a clear thesis, or main point. There should then be 2-3 body, or example, paragraphs. Each of these paragraphs should have their own, distinct theme. There should then be a concluding paragraph that ties up your ideas and then suggests what comes next. For example, if you wrote about how to improve your school, maybe you could finish up by describing how these changes could help other schools as well.

   If you chose the creative topic, there should still be structure to your story. There needs to be a problem, which builds to a climax, and then a resolution. Since you only have two pages and 25 minutes to get this done, you should know your problem before you begin to write.

2. **Word choice**

   Use descriptive language. Don't describe anything as "nice" or "good". Tell us specifically why something is nice or good. Better yet, show us and don't tell us. For example, don't say that you would make the cafeteria nicer in your school, tell us how you would rearrange the tables to create greater class unity and improve nutritional selections in order to improve students' academic achievement.

Use transitions. When you switch ideas, use words such as however, but, although, and in contrast to. When you are continuing with an idea, use words such as furthermore, in addition, and in summation. Students who do not use transition words is one of the biggest complaints of English teachers, so show the reader that you know how to use them.

3. **Creativity and development of ideas**

It is not enough just to be able to fit your writing into the form that you were taught in school. These prompts are designed to show how you think. This is your chance to shine! For the creative prompts, this is your chance to come up with unique ideas. If you choose the essay topic, the readers will be looking more at how well you develop your ideas. Can you see the outcome of actions? Can you provide details that are both relevant to the essay and supportive of your thesis or main idea?

The writing sample is a place for you to showcase your writing skills. It is just one more piece of information that the admissions committee will use in making their decisions.

Made in the USA
Lexington, KY
28 September 2012